P9-DWK-225

NATURAL AMERICA

This edition belongs to

_____

DAVID MUENCH

PREPARED BY THE BOOK DIVISION
NATIONAL GEOGRAPHIC SOCIETY
WASHINGTON, D.C.

NATURAL AMERICA

....

by TH Watkins

SNOW-COVERED BRANCHES *in a grove of Colorado aspens herald the coming of winter even as autumn color clings to trees in the background. Interludes in Colorado's national forests—or anywhere in the*

PAUL CHESLEY

national lands of the Rocky Mountain region, from Idaho to New Mexico—revive the human spirit at any time of year.

NATURAL AMERICA

By T.H. Watkins

Published by
The National Geographic Society

Reg Murphy, *President and
    Chief Executive Officer*
Gilbert M. Grosvenor,
    Chairman of the Board
Nina D. Hoffman,
    Senior Vice President

Prepared by
The Book Division

William R. Gray, *Vice President
    and Director*
Charles Kogod, *Assistant Director*
Barbara A. Payne,
    *Editorial Director and
    Managing Editor*
David Griffin, *Design Director*

Staff for this book

John Agnone, *Project Editor and
    Illustrations Editor*
Roberta R. Conlan, *Text Editor*
Suez B. Kehl, *Art Director*
Marianne Koszorus, *Consulting Art Director*
Anne E. Withers, *Researcher*
Peyton H. Moss, Jr., *Contributing Writer*
Lewis R. Bassford, *Production
    Project Manager*
Richard S. Wain, *Production*
Meredith C. Wilcox,
    Illustrations Assistant
Peggy Candore, Kevin G. Craig,
    Dale-Marie Herring, *Staff Assistants*

Manufacturing and Quality Control
George V. White, *Director*
John T. Dunn, *Associate Director*
Vincent P. Ryan, *Manager*
Polly P. Tompkins, *Executive Assistant*

Mark A. Wentling, *Indexer*

Copyright © 1998 National Geographic Society. All rights reserved. Reproduction of the whole or any part of the contents without written permission is prohibited. Library of Congress ℭℙ Data: page 200

PAGE 1: SURGING WITH POWER, *the Colorado River foams past the red cliffs of Marble Canyon in Grand Canyon National Park, Arizona. The river itself carved this many-storied gash in the earth over millions of years, just as it carved the rest of the wondrous maze of the Grand Canyon.*
PAGES 2-3: THE SUNRISE REFLECTION *of Alaska's Mount McKinley—at 20,320 feet the highest peak in North America—shimmers on the surface of Wonder Lake in Denali National Park and Preserve. A place of outsized marvels, Denali is only one of countless breathtaking sites preserved in the 630 million acres of parks, forests, refuges, and other national lands that are America's greatest natural legacy.*
PAGES 2-3: CARR CLIFTON/MINDEN PICTURES

CONTENTS

FERNS AND ALPINE DAISIES
brighten a rocky crevice beside the
lacy veil of Palisade Falls in Gallatin
National Forest, Montana.

SALVATORE VASAPOLLI

Just Beyond Your Front Door

ARID **TERRAIN** PEOPLED BY CACTUSES AND
FRINGE-TOED LIZARDS, LUSH TREE FERN FORESTS THAT
SHELTER RARE SPECIES OF BIRDS, FORBIDDING BADLANDS
SCULPTED BY EONS OF WIND AND WATER, AND QUIET
WOODED TRAILS THAT SOOTHE THE SPIRIT—ALL BELONG
TO THE COLLECTIVE NATIONAL HERITAGE THAT LIES
JUST BEYOND YOUR FRONT DOOR.

• •

DESERT MARKINGS: *The Providence Mountains in California's Mojave National Preserve provide a misty backdrop for a cluster of barrel cactuses (opposite). A spiral petroglyph in Saguaro National Park, Arizona (above), evokes the presence of its ancient makers.*

TOM BEAN (OPPOSITE); DENNIS FLAHERTY (ABOVE)

GLEAMING WHITE AGAINST *the Pacific Northwest sky, the snow-blanketed slopes of 9,131-foot-high Mount Shuksan rise into heavy clouds to tower over silver fir and mountain hemlock in*

DAVID MUENCH

Washington's North Cascades National Park. Designated a national park in 1968, North Cascades adjoins two recreation areas; together these national lands units include more than 684,000 acres of alpine majesty.

I WAS BORN AND REARED in the San Bernardino Valley of southern California, 70 miles east of downtown Los Angeles, surrounded by orange groves, mountains, and deserts. Given the valley's semiarid climate we had more in common with western states like Arizona and Nevada than we did with any part of California north of the Tehachapi Mountains.

It was a western place, this long valley, and close to Edenic. At least, that is how I remember it, my memories speaking with the voice of a ten-year-old boy. The San Bernardino range, darkly mantled in ponderosa and Jeffrey pines, ran like a long blue wall from San Bernardino Mountain all the way to Mount Baldy and the beginning of the San Gabriel Mountains. In those days, some 50 years ago, there was still plenty of water coming out of the annual snowpack of the mountains, local springs, and the groundwater table to satisfy a population that had not yet begun to eradicate the orange groves that gave the valley its character and most of its income. Smog was only an ugly rumor until after World War II, even in Los Angeles, and it would be more than another decade after that before an ocher-colored smudge on the western horizon would sometimes slowly creep eastward to engulf our space. There was space, and light, and air that was filled with the heady essence of oranges.

Above all, just over the mountains through Cajon Pass was the Mojave Desert, with its enormous distances and a dun-colored landscape touched here and there by ghostly shades of pink and yellow, lavender and blue, maroon and gray, all from a palette of colors grown delicate with age. The Mojave's cactus gardens, Joshua tree forests, and palm oases lived among sinuous sharp-edged sand dunes, cinder cones, and broken old mountains rising like the bones of ancient monsters out of the wide alluvial plains.

My mother and father loved the desert. They would pile the family into our bulbous 1939 nine-passenger Buick—the six children packed like puppies in a box—and climb over the mountains to the Mojave. In those expeditions, I learned the desert with single-minded dedication. Climbing to the top of some rocky eminence, I could see spread out below me more land than I ever thought existed in the world. Scrambling around in gullies, some deep enough to be called a "canyon," I discovered tiny springs surrounded by ferns and mosses, their pools teeming with pollywogs and minnows and swept by the bright punctuation of dragonflies. I saw deer browsing in the chaparral and jackrabbits scampering from shade to shade among the creosote bushes. I caught horned lizards and took them home and once even captured a desert tortoise, though it shames me to remember it, now that the creature is a threatened species. Back then, nearly everyone I knew had a tortoise lurking in their backyard, chewing up lettuce leaves with reptilian gravity. I collected rocks and explored abandoned mines, and in wet springtimes I marveled at the carpets of tiny desert flowers whose colors challenged spectrographic analysis. As a child will, I accepted this first wilderness without question; I took it as my own.

It was nearly 20 years before I learned how right I had been in my innocence. In more than simply the metaphorical sense, this bright country just beyond my front door belonged to me. I owned it, as did my mother and father and brothers and sisters and every single American. Most of the Mojave is owned by all of us and managed by federal agencies of the United States. It is just one small part of the American public lands system—the national lands held in trust by the federal government for the American people in perpetuity. Though I didn't know it then, my childhood playground was part of what may have been the most important inheritance ever given any people at any time.

"In the United States," the poet Gertrude Stein once wrote, "there is more space where nobody is than where anybody is. This is what makes America what it is." Not ordinarily given to musings regarding the American landscape, Stein was very close to the mark. To many historians, land was the principal catalyst in the formation of the nation's character and institutions. The dimensions of space that lay before us gave us the dimensions of our freedom—freedom of movement, freedom of opportunity, the freedom, finally, to dream. Historian Bernard DeVoto, for example, wrote, "Ours is a story mad with the impossible, it is by chaos out of dream, it began as dream and it has continued as dream down to the last headlines you read in a newspaper." This dream, of course, came at the expense of those who inhabited the land before Europeans arrived. The treatment of Native Americans at the hands of an ever westering and land-hungry Republic still rankles the memory, on both sides.

Still, however ugly and often vicious it was, the westering process made these United States a continental nation. Within that continent, the dream of opportunity was played out with an almost frenzied abandon—"Full speed ahead and damn the tomorrows," in the phrase of western historian Ray Allen Billington. In the more than two centuries since the westering first crossed through the Appalachian Mountains into the valley of the Ohio River, the land has been largely given away or eaten up by urban sprawl or corrupted by extractive enterprises such as hardrock mining, logging, and cattle and sheep grazing. Much of the natural integrity that gave the land and its wild creatures their value in the first place was lost.

Not all of it was lost, however. What this nation had the good sense to set aside, even in the midst of determined exploitation, is still so abundant and beautiful and various that it is unmatched by any other nation on the planet. If one takes in all the land from American Samoa to Puerto Rico, Florida to Alaska, Maine to California, there are today more than 630 million acres of national lands in the United States, nearly a million square miles of plains and deserts, mountains and jungles, and rivers, lakes, and seashores—and all the habitats and wildlife they contain.

THIS IS NOT TO SAY that we always appreciate, or even know, what we have. A man from Springfield in southern Missouri, going out with his guns and bird dogs on a fall morning, may not know that the woods he is hunting in are part of Mark Twain National Forest. A woman from Corpus Christi, Texas, casting her line into the surf on Padre Island, will take her catch from the waters of a national seashore. A birder peering through dune grasses to spy on a piping plover on Plum Island, an hour or so out of Boston, may be unaware that the bird is nesting in Parker River National Wildlife Refuge. And a rock climber from Los Angeles, testing the towering boulders in the Granite Mountains of the East Mojave, may not know that he is enjoying his rugged sport in one of the nation's newest national preserves.

Moreover, it is easy to get confused over what a federal public land unit is in the first place. For example, Baxter State Park in Maine and Canyonlands National Park in Utah are both public lands open to everyone. However, the management and fate of Baxter State Park is in the hands of that state's people alone—just as a municipal park is controlled by the city that owns it or a county park is run by the county. But Utah's Canyonlands is part of the federal public lands; its fate is a matter in which every American—including those in Maine—has a legitimate interest. Every citizen has an equal right to try to influence the decisions that govern the management of federal public lands by the federal agency appointed to do the job; in Canyonlands's case, the agency is the National Park Service. Canyonlands is everybody's park, as is Yellowstone, or Great Smoky Mountains. And Chippewa National Forest in Minnesota is everybody's forest, and Great Swamp National Wildlife Refuge in New Jersey is everybody's national wildlife refuge.

Millions of Americans grow up in this citizenship of land without giving it much more thought than they do such other distinctly American privileges as the Bill of Rights. This lack of thought is dangerous, both to the land itself and to its preservation for our children's children. As ecologist and wilderness advocate Aldo Leopold wrote in a famous essay on the land ethic, "All ethics so far evolved rest upon a single premise: that the individual is a member of a community of interdependent parts."

Leopold enlarged the concept of community to include "soils, waters, plants, and animals, or collectively: the land" and declared a new role for humanity: "In short," he wrote, " a land ethic changes the role of *Homo sapiens* from conqueror of the land-community to plain member and citizen of it. It implies respect for his fellow-members, and also respect for the community as such."

The citizenship of land, like the citizenship of the social con-tract that binds us with the Constitution, carries with it responsi-bilities as well as rights. This stewardship recognizes that our inheritance must be not only celebrated but also watched over and cared for. Although the greatest portion of the "land com-munity" that remains to us is in the national lands, even these are under pressure from population growth, urban expansion, auto-mobile use, and, in some areas, the kind of careless management and exploitation that has brought so much of the land to ruin.

We must give these lands the best we have to give of protec-tion and, where appropriate, preservation, so that we can pass on an inheritance as healthy as we can possibly make it. Just as the children of today cannot be allowed to take now-rare desert tor-toises from the sands of the Mojave, we must accept our respon-sibility to the fellow members of the land community. We cannot afford to continue the game of sacrificing the future for the sake of present gain. We know too much now about what can be lost.

In that spirit, this book hopes to give you a sense of just how rich and various the national lands are, and how important they are to all Americans, no matter where we live. Along the way I also wish to help you understand where the lands came from, what their problems are today, and what they may face in the near future. Finally, I hope you will come away with a clear grasp of what is being done—and, more important, what needs to be done—to ensure that in fifty or a hundred years our fellow citizens will have reason to thank us.

FOLLOWING PAGES: *A weathered granite arch in Inyo National Forest frames the knife-edged wintry peaks of the eastern Sierra Nevada. Formed some 25 million years ago when continental plates collided just west of the Great Basin Desert, the Sierra stretch in a huge, broken wall for 400 miles. About half of the range is managed by the U.S. Forest Service and more than three-quarters of it is desig-nated federal land.*

DAVID MUENCH

In the Eye of the Beholder

WHETHER THEY EMBRACE THE COOL
WATERS OF THE OCEAN OR
SUN-BLISTERED DESERT SANDS,
THE NATIONAL LANDS ARE TREASURES
WHOSE VARIED BEAUTY LIES
IN THE EYE OF THE BEHOLDER.

• •

FROM EAST TO WEST: *Morning sunlight casts a pink glow on the rocky shoreline of Maine's Acadia National Park (opposite). In California's Death Valley National Park, the scorched desert floor blisters into alkali plates, which stretch nearly to the horizon (above).* 19

DAVID MUENCH (BOTH)

PIERCED BY THE WHITE SHAFT OF BRIDALVEIL FALL, *the cloud-roofed valley of Yosemite National Park in the Sierra Nevada is relatively young, geologically speaking.*

DAVID MUENCH

"In the few tens of thousands of years of stormy cultivation they have been blest with," wrote John Muir of the Sierra a century ago, "how beautiful they have become!"

ONE SUMMER DAY in Alaska several years ago, I was flown in a bush plane from Fairbanks north into the watershed of the Yukon River. As the White Mountains dropped behind us, we passed over Yukon Flats National Wildlife Refuge, a huge plain that stretches a hundred miles across from the White Mountains to the Brooks Range. Below us, the great river gleamed like polished silver on its nearly 2,000-mile journey from Canada's Yukon Territory to the Bering Sea. As it braids its way through thousands of square miles of boreal forest, the river passes stands of black spruce, balsam poplar, alder, and birch. The sight of the river alone was worth the trip, but it was more than matched by the view of what must have been thousands of ponds, dotting the land on both sides of the Yukon. They spread as far as the eye could see, each a different size and shape, glittering shards of reflected sunlight. Pointing to the sight, I tapped the pilot on the shoulder and shouted over the roar of the engine. "How many of them are there?"

"Damned if I know," he yelled back, looking at me as if I had lost my senses. "Never thought to count 'em."

When I think of the national lands, I think of all those pools of light, for the lands are not a single entity but many units, each as brightly important as any other. Sorting out the units' various, and sometimes multiple, designations under the national lands system —to say nothing of which federal body is responsible for their administration—requires a certain patience. To start with, the 630 million acres include hundreds of individual units that range in size from a few acres to several million acres. In geography they vary from tropical islands to waterless deserts, and in character from nearly untouched wilderness to areas sometimes so full of people you could mistake them for small cities. The lands also serve different purposes, from resource production to the preservation of natural diversity.

It would be simpler—and maybe better—if the entire complex were under the administration of a single government body— a Department of Conservation. Indeed, one Secretary of the Interior, Harold L. Ickes, tried to persuade both President Franklin Roosevelt and the Congress to restructure the Executive Branch with just that end in mind. He failed, however, and the national lands remain divided between the Department of the Interior and the Department of Agriculture, each of which further divides responsibility among a plethora of smaller agencies and offices.

In addition to their status as national lands, many sites within the national lands system are given two other forms of protection. One is designation as a wilderness area. As stipulated by the Wilderness Act of 1964, these are regions whose natural values and beauty are considered so significant that all vehicles, commercial activities, and permanent recreation development—buildings, roads, campgrounds, and so forth—are prohibited. The only recreational activities allowed are day hiking, backpacking, horse-packing, canoeing, hunting, and fishing. Some 650 individual sites have been deemed wilderness areas. They range in size from Florida's Pelican Island National Wildlife Refuge, scarcely more than two acres, to the nine million acres in Wrangell-St. Elias National Park and Preserve in Alaska.

The other designation applies to rivers. The national lands are laced by river segments classified as "wild," "scenic," or "recreational," each classification determined by the degree of road access and development along the designated stretches. In Montana, 149 undeveloped miles of the Missouri River curving through lands administered by the Bureau of Land Management have been given one of these designations, as have 83 miles of the Tuolumne as it passes through Stanislaus National Forest in California's Sierra Nevada. Along all of these protected river segments, whatever their designation, dams and other habitat-damaging activities are controlled or prohibited outright to keep the rivers free-flowing and to preserve the remarkable or outstanding characteristic that warranted the Wild and Scenic nomination. Five rivers have also won special classification as national rivers, a category administered by the National Park Service. National rivers are declared by an act of Congress that specifies the goals and values of the individual river park; thus, allowable activities vary from one national river park to another.

Finally, many of the national lands provide routes for units of the National Trails System. In the East, for example, is the Appalachian Trail, running more than 2,100 miles from Georgia to Maine along the Appalachian Mountains. The Continental Divide Trail covers 3,200 miles from Mexico to Canada along the spine of the Rocky Mountains. And on the West Coast, the Pacific Crest Trail runs nearly 2,640 miles through the Sierra Nevada and Cascade ranges to the Canadian border.

The Department of the Interior administers most of the national lands system—about 439 million acres. Of this, the National Park Service manages 83 million acres, including 54 national parks, 16 national preserves, 19 national recreation areas, 73 national monuments, 10 national seashores, and 4 national lakeshores.

The National Park Service also supervises many national historical parks, battlefields, battlefield parks, battlefield sites, military parks, memorials, historic sites, and a handful of

DAVID MUENCH

miscellaneous additional sites. However, since the purpose of these units is not primarily to sustain their natural values, none will be included in this discussion.

National recreation areas tend to serve mixed purposes. Many, like Lake Mead National Recreation Area (NRA) behind Hoover Dam in Nevada, have been set aside to provide fishing, boating, swimming, and other recreational opportunities at federal reservoirs. Others, like Golden Gate NRA in the San Francisco Bay Area, are available for camping but are also dedicated to the preservation of historic sites like the San Francisco Presidio. Still others, like Santa Monica Mountains NRA in California or Glen Canyon NRA in Utah, are heavily used for all kinds of recreational activities but also preserve large natural landscapes. National seashores and national lakeshores, for their part, are generally so designated to preserve natural areas. However, some, like Cape

Cod National Seashore in Massachusetts, often resemble recreation areas, particularly on a crowded summer day at the beach.

Where the greatest puzzlement tends to arise, however, is between and among national parks, national preserves, and national monuments. What distinguishes one from another? First, a national preserve allows hunting, as in Big Cypress National Preserve in Florida or Mojave National Preserve in California; in the national parks, hunting is banned. Second, national parks and preserves are, by law, created to encompass large and complex areas of natural landscape and habitat. The six-million-acre Denali National Park and Preserve in Alaska, for example, includes Mount McKinley and the Alaska Range, and a subarctic landscape of tundra and taiga, as well as grizzlies, caribou, wolves, moose, and Dall sheep. Similarly, the 77,109-acre Great Basin National Park in Nevada, sandwiched between the Rockies and the Sierra Nevada, includes plant communities that range from sagebrush desert to alpine meadows as well as limestone caves and the only glacier in the area. National parks and national preserves can be established only by an act of Congress and both are under the supervision of the National Park Service.

NATIONAL MONUMENTS may also be established by Congress, but the President can establish a national monument by invoking the Antiquities Act of 1906. Theodore Roosevelt did so in designating Grand Canyon National Monument in Arizona in 1908. (It later was redesignated a national park, as many monuments have been.) President Bill Clinton invoked the act when he established Grand Staircase-Escalante National Monument in Utah in 1996. And while some national monuments do preserve large landscapes, many are set aside to protect only a single natural site, or archaeological ruins. Grand Staircase-Escalante, for instance, is 1.7 million acres in size, but Rainbow Bridge in Utah encompasses only 160 acres, and the pueblo ruins in Hovenweep on the Colorado-Utah border contain 784 acres. Some national monuments are administered by other agencies—a handful by the Department of Agriculture and one—Grand Staircase-Escalante—by the Bureau of Land Management.

The National Park System holds some of the greatest "icons" in the nation's collection of natural treasures, places like Yosemite or Yellowstone or the Everglades or the Grand Canyon and others that are generally known and admired by much of the world. For many people, those powerful landscapes embody everything that

STALKS OF REED CANARY *grass ring the marshy shores of Pilgrim Lake in Cape Cod National Seashore in Massachusetts. Like most eastern parks, this one was cobbled together by the federal acquisition of private and state lands. As Secretary of Interior Stewart Udall told Congress in 1961, "The plants and wildlife that mingle on Cape Cod in unusual variety give the area outstanding biological significance." Congress agreed and authorized the seashore later that year.*

comes to mind when they say the words "national park" and start planning next year's vacation.

Yosemite National Park, for example, is a kind of natural fantasy, with broad mountain meadows ringed by endless groves of ponderosa pines, towering glacier-scoured walls, and waterfalls that take the breath away every time you see them. Encountering it for the first time as you emerge from the tunnel on the Wawona Road can be so deeply moving an experience that it burns the sight in memory, a photograph that refuses to fade. I was maybe 20 years old when it happened to me, and to this day I can hear the gasp I uttered at the sight.

YELLOWSTONE inspires similar reactions, as do Grand Teton and the Grand Canyon and other much-visited parks such as Zion, Rocky Mountain, and Great Smoky Mountains. But one can find diversity of geology, geography, habitat, wildlife, and scenic vistas in other holdings of the National Park System as well. The wave-sculpted coast of Maine's Acadia National Park, for example, stands as one of the most dramatic meetings of land and sea to be found anywhere in the world. The state of Washington's Olympic National Park has moist, temperate rain forests whose sheer weight of life—from the microbes in the richly populated soil to the rising glory of 800-year-old Douglas firs—is almost incalculable. Yes, Arizona's Grand Canyon, carved down through rocks more than 1.5 billion years old, can leave the imagination gasping, but canoeing through Minnesota's Voyageurs National Park, with its blue lakes, dark forested islands, and cloud-navigated skies, can bring serenity to the heart. In the light-stabbed groves of Redwood National Park in northern California, the *Sequoia sempervirens* rise like tens of thousands of exclamation points, many more than 250 feet high. From the eerie "badlands" of El Malpais National Monument in western New Mexico and the enormous stump-like upthrust of Devils Tower National Monument in northeastern Wyoming, to the sculptured stone formations in Pictured Rocks National Lakeshore on Lake Superior, the treasures of the National Park System are, in the words of one 19th-century hotel promoter, "scenes of wonder and curiosity."

The other large category of national lands over which the Department of the Interior holds sway is the National Wildlife Refuge System, administered by the department's U.S. Fish and Wildlife Service (USFWS). Some 92 million acres of national wildlife refuges are divided among 511 individual units, each established primarily for the protection of plant and animal species. Many of these species are members of, or candidates for, the endangered and threatened lists that both the USFWS and many states maintain under the stipulations of the Endangered Species Act of 1973, which mandates special protection and recovery plans. The refuges are also administered so that individual units may allow certain uses that have been deemed "compatible" with species and habitat protection. However, the compatibility of activities such as farming, mining, oil and gas extraction, hunting, fishing, and other recreational pursuits, from scuba diving to jet skiing, is a matter of debate, and the policy has come under increasing criticism from scientists and environmentalists.

In size, variety, and drama of its individual units, the National Wildlife Refuge System holds its own against the National Park System. The Arctic National Wildlife Refuge in the northeastern corner of Alaska, for example, is 19 million acres designated to protect tens of thousands of migrating caribou, as well as Dall sheep, arctic wolves, grizzlies, polar bears, musk oxen, and hundreds of thousands of resident and migratory birds, including snow geese, arctic terns, old-squaw ducks, phalaropes, and ptarmigans. To stand on the banks of the Hulahula River as it emerges from its U-shaped valley in the Brooks Range into the coastal plain is to experience a sense of vastness that enlarges the spirit. Just behind you loom knife-edged peaks of a range that runs 600 miles from east to west across most of the top quarter of Alaska. Spreading out before you, the brown rolling tundra of the coastal plain winks with tiny multicolored arctic flowers and lichen-splashed stones. Glinting in the sun, the racing river is so loaded with glacial silt that even the rapids look gray. Twenty or thirty miles to the north, if you are far enough out on the plain or high enough on a rise, you might spy the shimmering white vacancy of the Beaufort Sea's ice pack; the wind driving in off that pack could be coming to you all the way from the North Pole, because there is nothing for more than a thousand miles to stand in its way.

Alaska has the biggest refuges in the system. Kodiak Refuge on Kodiak and Afognak Islands, for example, contains 1.5 million acres where, during spawning season, the densest population of Alaska brown bears in the world can be seen slapping fat salmon out of tumbling streams. Farther north, Yukon Delta Refuge pokes its 19.6-million-acre nose into the Bering Sea. The lower forty-eight have a few big refuges, too. Cabeza Prieta Refuge on the Arizona-Mexico border, for instance, has 860,000 acres designated for the protection of saguaro, organ pipe, cholla, and other species of cactus typical of the Sonoran (Continued on page 39)

FOLLOWING PAGES:
Prickly pear cactuses blanket a field in Big Bend National Park in Texas, where sunlight paints a blush on the high peaks of the Chisos Mountains. Located in the heart of the Chihuahuan Desert, the park is home to more than 45 species of cactuses, and contains some of the most rugged country to be found along the Rio Grand River between Texas and Mexico.

CARR CLIFTON/MINDEN PICTURES

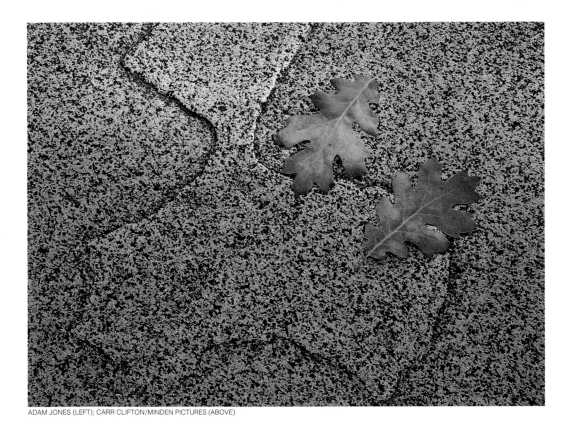

ADAM JONES (LEFT); CARR CLIFTON/MINDEN PICTURES (ABOVE)

GOLDEN ORNAMENTS FOR THE GOLDEN STATE—

Horsetail Fall in California's Yosemite National Park plunges like a string of gold down glacier-carved walls at sunset (opposite), and autumn oak leaves rest like gilded ornaments on a granite slab (above) in Plumas National Forest in the northern Sierra Nevada. Inspired no doubt by scenes like these, John Muir declared the Sierra the "Range of Light, surely the brightest and best of all the Lord has built . . . ."

GLACIER-FED WELLS CREEK in Mount Baker-Snoqualmie National Forest in Washington
threads its way through dense stands of old-growth forest. The ancient forests of the Pacific Northwest—

PETER ESSICK

only small remnants of which remain uncut in the national forests of the region—are a complex habitat that is extraordinarily rich in species diversity, including Douglas firs up to 800 years old.

A SOLITARY CONIFER
*decorates a snowy pocket in Colorado's
San Juan National Forest, a national lands
preserve covering nearly two million acres
of aspen, spruce, and ponderosa pine
forests in the San Juan Mountains.*

PAUL CHESLEY

LIKE TWO PIECES *of a jigsaw puzzle, snowy ledges created by geological uplift, tilting, and erosion bracket a tree-covered valley in Jedediah Smith Wilderness Area in Targhee National Forest, on the*

PAUL CHESLEY

western slopes of the Teton Range. Targhee is part of a 14-million-acre ecosystem in Wyoming, Idaho, and Montana that includes two parks, all or part of seven national forests, and three national wildlife refuges.

SALVATORE VASAPOLLI

desert ecosystem. The refuge also protects desert bighorn sheep, threatened desert tortoises, and endangered Sonoran pronghorn; in the United States, the pronghorn can be found only in Cabeza Prieta, in adjacent Organ Pipe Cactus National Monument, and in Barry M. Goldwater Air Force Range in Arizona.

Most refuges, however, show up as little more than dots and smudges on the map. Despite their modest size, each is crucial to the preservation of one or more species, many of them endangered or threatened. The 12,838 acres of Nevada's Ash Meadows Refuge, for example, offer protection to speckled dace and Devils Hole pupfish. Crocodiles are protected in Florida's Crocodile Lake Refuge, the California clapper rail in that state's San Francisco Bay Refuge. Iowa's portion of the Upper Mississippi River National Wildlife and Fish Refuge offers sanctuary to dozens of migratory species along the Mississippi flyway, and the 7,122 acres of Montezuma Refuge in New York's Finger Lakes region do the same for species in the Atlantic flyway. In Montana, the Red Rock Lakes Refuge provides crucial year-round habitat for trumpeter swans; tiny endangered key deer find a home in National Key Deer Refuge in the Florida Keys; and sandhill cranes do their oddly graceful mating dance in the many "pothole" refuges—prairie bogs and ponds—that dot North Dakota. For these and hundreds of other plants and animals, the units of the National Wildlife Refuge System are not merely sanctuaries, they are an archipelago of life.

THE DEPARTMENT OF THE INTERIOR'S final share in the national inheritance of land has been called various things at various times, officially and unofficially. For decades, these 264 million acres were described merely as the "public lands," the only chunk of the original public domain that had not been sold, given away, or converted into national parks, refuges, and forests. During his tenure between 1961 and 1969, Secretary of Interior Stewart Udall renamed them the "national resource lands" in an attempt to give them a little more panache.

In this book we will refer to them as the Bureau of Land Management or BLM lands to distinguish them from the rest of the national lands system. Every western state, including Alaska, has some BLM lands. Almost 70 percent of Nevada, for instance—nearly 49 million acres—is designated BLM land. In Utah, the numbers are a little over 22 million acres—almost 42 percent of the state. Much of this land has been or is being heavily developed. Cattle and sheep grazing are still the dominant use of BLM

LOW-LYING MIST *traces the contours of the Snake River as it wends its way below the majestic peaks of Grand Teton National Park at Jackson Hole, Wyoming (opposite). Established in 1929, the park at first included only the crags of the Teton Range but was enlarged in 1950 by the addition of rolling grasslands along the Snake. The expansion was made possible by the donation of Jackson Hole lands by John D. Rockefeller, Jr., who had spent years buying up private land in the valley for just this purpose.*

lands in many states, and there is also mining, particularly in places like northern Nevada. In addition, although not much of the BLM lands is forested, the bureau manages about 50 million acres of timber. Despite all of this development, hundreds of places within BLM lands are as ecologically significant and aesthetically satisfying as any in the nation, and, although they are sometimes called "the lands no one knows," their beauty and variety are becoming better recognized every year.

Given that my introduction to the enchantments of the natural world came largely from BLM lands, I confess to a special fondness for them. This love has only grown over the last 35 years as I've tramped around in them and written about them, from the Nigu River Valley of northern Alaska to the San Pedro River of southern Arizona, from the High Plains of northeastern Montana to the Black Rock Desert of Nevada. Wherever I have gone, I have been struck by how profoundly important these lands are to the whole network of the national lands system. They provide geographic links between and hugely important adjuncts to national parks, national wildlife refuges, and national forests all over the West, serving to keep these preserves from being completely isolated "land islands," which would make their plant and animal species even more vulnerable to pressure on all sides from development and human population growth.

ASIDE FROM THEIR IMPORTANCE as a kind of natural "matrix" for much of the rest of the national lands system, the BLM lands themselves contain hundreds of sites as deserving of protection as any other part of the national landscape. BLM lands in southern Utah, for example, virtually surround Arches, Canyonlands, Capitol Reef, Zion, and Bryce Canyon National Parks, as well as Glen Canyon National Recreation Area and three national forests—Dixie, Fishlake, and Manti-La Sal. If you drive over Boulder Mountain on Utah Highway 12 through Dixie National Forest between the hamlets of Boulder and Torrey, you can stop off at a scenic overlook and gaze over the lumpy red-rock formations of Capitol Reef National Park. In the distance you'd see the Henry Mountains, unsuccessful volcanoes poking their often snow-covered heads from a canyon-cut sea of desert mesas the color of a lion's flank. These are BLM lands. Or you could go into the San Rafael Swell, just off Utah Highway 24, and lose yourself in a maze of stark, rust-colored buttes, deep slot canyons hardly wider than your shoulders, and stone formations that beg human comparisons. Here, sagebrush flats and table mountains call up memories of every western movie you ever saw. "Sinbad Country," they call some of the Swell for its magical character. It is also BLM country.

If you leave Interstate 70 and drive a long dirt road out to the Wedge Overlook, you can step to the lip of the precipice and look down on intricate canyons that are the handiwork of the meandering San Rafael River cutting through eons of what is now BLM lands geology. Or go back to Highway 12, get out, and leave your car at the highway bridge across the Escalante River. Hike a few miles along the river between slickrock walls to a parklike area called Death Hollow. Crowded with cottonwoods and big sage, populated by nearly invisible herdlets of mule deer, walled in by red Navajo sandstone streaked with purple-black smears, this is part of Grand Staircase-Escalante National Monument—a BLM lands monument.

Head over to Utah Highway 95 one afternoon and take the dirt road across a rolling tableland of dark green sage and red earth to Burr Point. Stand at the lip of the land and, while the sun slides down the sky behind you, look out over 20 miles of canyons cut into layer after layer of red-rock sandstones and shales and conglomerates by the Dirty Devil River 1,500 feet below you. Then try to convince yourself that you are not at the Grand Canyon.

These and dozens of similar sites on BLM land, almost six million acres, have been identified by environmentalists as candidates for the National Wilderness Preservation System in Utah. There is precedent for such an idea. With passage of the Arizona Desert Wilderness Act in 1990, more than 1.1 million acres of BLM land in Arizona were designated wilderness. Four years later, Congress passed the California Desert Protection Act, which designated 3.5 million acres of new BLM wilderness and established 1.4-million-acre Mojave National Preserve. The act also enlarged Joshua Tree and Death Valley National Monuments, upgrading both monuments to the status of national parks.

When we turn to lands administered by the Department of Agriculture, we find the second largest contingent of national lands—187.2 million acres of national forests and 4.2 million acres of national grasslands managed by the U.S. Forest Service. Every state in the nation except Connecticut, Rhode Island, Massachusetts, New Jersey, Maryland, Delaware, and Iowa has one or more units of national forest within its borders. Some states have several forests. California, for instance, has 18 forests and 1 grassland, and Colorado has 12 forests and 2 grasslands. Twelve states also have one or more national grasslands.

There are very few major American population centers from which a national forest can't be reached with relative ease. New Yorkers can escape the towers and concrete of Manhattan and in a few hours be walking a trail through the shadowed mix of life in Green Mountain National Forest in Vermont or White Mountain

JIM BRANDENBURG/MINDEN PICTURES

National Forest in New Hampshire and Maine. Here, the city dweller can find a riot of diverse plant life, from trillium, lady's slipper, pitcher plant, and fringed orchid to alternate-leaved dogwood, paper birch, and Canada yew. These forests also hold eastern hemlock, red and sugar maples, oak, and pine—especially the elegant, towering white pine. At the highest elevations are needle-leaved spruce-fir forests—balsam fir and red spruce.

Atlantans can head out to Chattahoochee National Forest and tramp up and down the rolling old mountains of the southern Appalachians to find another vegetative porridge. This one features yellow poplar, eastern hemlock, blackgum, butternut, black walnut, black cherry, American beech, white pine, and oak. The forest floor is lumpy with moss-covered decomposing logs, above which grow flowering dogwood and white ash, yellow buckeye and sourwood, and several species of magnolia. Thickets of rhododendron and mountain laurel are interspersed with maidenhair and lady ferns, spicebush and wild geranium, Carolina silverbell and highbush blueberry.

The citizens of Minneapolis can similarly enjoy the delights of Chippewa National Forest in northern Minnesota, and denizens of Chicago can easily get to Wisconsin's Nicolet National Forest. Residents of Denver can be in Arapaho National Forest within a matter of minutes, and the inhabitants of Phoenix have swift access to Prescott National Forest to the north or one of the several scattered units of Coronado National Forest to the south.

In Portland, Oregon, Mount Hood National Forest begins practically in the city's backyard, and millions of Californians can hardly turn in any direction without running into a national forest. San Bernardino National Forest lies in the mountains between the Mojave Desert and Greater Los Angeles, Los Padres National Forest in the chaparral-covered coast range between the San Joaquin Valley and the Pacific Ocean, and no fewer than eight national forests are located in the Sierra Nevada.

The forests also have a special place in American history. It was the forests that the European settlers of the early 17th century encountered first, the forests where we learned to make our way on this new continent. The forests were cleared to provide for a growing populace, their timber stripped to make ships and houses, their soils converted to cropland. Later, as that populace spread across the Appalachian Mountains into the Ohio River Valley and then all the way to the Mississippi, the trees were so systematically harvested that, from Wisconsin to the Carolinas, virtually none of the original forests were left by the latter third of the 19th century. But it was then, just at the point when the forests of the Rocky Mountains were being assaulted, that the conservation movement in this country truly began. And it is in the forests today, from the remaining second- and third-growth woods of the southern Appalachians to the fast-vanishing ponderosa pine groves of the Rocky Mountains and the dense old growth of the Pacific Northwest, that much of the conservation effort is being concentrated.

The national lands, in short, are a geographic montage, as complex in their natural values as they are in their bureaucratic management. As an organized, protected system, the lands are unique to the United States and the legitimate source of much national pride. If our past has been shaped to a great extent by what the land has given us, our future, as novelist and historian Wallace Stegner believed, can only be sustained if we give something back in the way of protection. "It would promise us a more serene and confident future," Stegner wrote, "if, at the start of our sixth century of residence in America, we began to listen to the land, and hear what it says, and know what it can and cannot do."

RANKS OF FIRE
in a controlled burn sweep across a remnant of tallgrass prairie owned by the Nature Conservancy in Oklahoma (opposite). Private organizations have helped many such lands become part of the national lands system, including parts of Tallgrass Prairie National Preserve in neighboring Kansas. Controlled burns are designed to mimic the natural fires that remove soil-covering litter, release nutrients, and stimulate the growth of native grasses.

FOLLOWING PAGES:
Within a few years of a burn, whether caused by lightning or controlled by man, regrowth can produce a rich landscape like that of Grand River National Grassland in South Dakota.

TOM BEAN

VIEWED FROM THE PRECIPITOUS LIP OF LOWER FALLS, *the Yellowstone River plunges down the Grand Canyon of the Yellowstone in Wyoming's Yellowstone National Park. Seeping*

PAUL CHESLEY

hot water from geothermal activity long ago combined with minerals to paint the gray and brown rock of the canyon walls with tinges of red, orange, pink, and yellow—the color that gave the river its name.

PAUL CHESLEY

ADAM JONES

BISON ENVELOPED BY *the ghostly mists of geothermal vents in Yellowstone National Park come to drink at sunrise (above), while Old Faithful erupts in the background. The discovery of commercially valuable thermophiles, heat-loving microorganisms that live in the park's geothermal pools (left), has inspired medical and chemical companies to seek research permits from the Park Service to study the organisms. Within the park's thousands of geothermal features is a diversity of life that may rival that of the tropical rain forest. This extreme environment may offer new information about not only the origins of life on earth but also the possibility of life elsewhere in the universe.*

STRIATED SANDSTONE ARCH

forms a sturdy bridge across a red-rock alcove in the BLM lands of the Upper Gulch region in southern Utah's Escalante River canyons. Included in a presidential decree establishing the Grand Staircase-Escalante National Monument in 1996, the canyons are being proposed as an addition to the National Wilderness Preservation System by wilderness advocates.

DAVID MUENCH

**CARVING
ITS WAY**

*through several
hundred million years
of sedimentary rock,
the Colorado River
ties a watery knot
at Eightmile Bar in
Glen Canyon
National Recreation
Area in Arizona. Such
spectacular canyon
systems are typical
of BLM lands in
southern Utah.
Prickly fingers of
organ pipe cactus
(below) sprout from
a bed of brittlebrush
in Arizona's Organ
Pipe Cactus National
Monument.*

CARR CLIFTON/MINDEN PICTURES

DAVID MUENCH

A PALE MOON HOVERS *over the horizon of the Grand Canyon beyond the monumental formation called Wotans Throne, seen here from the North Rim. Arizona's Grand Canyon National Park,*

TOM BEAN

like Yosemite and Yellowstone, is one of the icons of the national lands system. Grand Canyon and Yosemite receive more than four million visitors a year, Yellowstone more than three million.

The Inheritance

The silken rush OF WOODLAND WATERS AND
THE SCOURED SHAPES OF THE DESERT—
THESE AND COUNTLESS OTHER TREASURES
WE OWE TO THOSE FARSIGHTED ENOUGH
TO HAVE PRESERVED THE PUBLIC LANDS
THAT MAKE UP OUR INHERITANCE.

....

HEMLOCK BRANCHES *frame Lewis Falls in Virginia's Shenandoah National Park (opposite), purchased with donations from many private citizens. On BLM lands in Utah, eons of erosion have turned rock into an otherworldly skeleton (above).*

57

DAVID MUENCH (OPPOSITE); TOM BEAN (ABOVE)

SEA AND SKY TRADE COLORS
in the morning light at Cape Hatteras
National Seashore, North Carolina.
Established in 1937 as the country's first
national seashore, Cape Hatteras today
is one of ten national seashores, seven
of them along the Atlantic coast.

DAVID MUENCH

T HAT THE NATIONAL LANDS SYSTEM even exists is remarkable, for it contradicts the dominant theme of our history: namely, that the vast and virgin territory spreading ever westward was there to be used— bought, sold, farmed, built upon, and otherwise put to the work of satisfying human needs and ambition. The obsession with the land began immediately. In describing what he found on the shores of Chesapeake Bay, John Smith, one of the founders and early leaders of Jamestown, wrote in *A Map of Virginia:*

> *". . . heaven and earth never agreed better to frame a place for mans habitation being of our constitutions, were it fully manured and inhabited by industrious people. Here are mountaines, hils, plaines, valleyes, rivers and brookes, all running most pleasantly into a faire Bay compassed but for the mouth with fruitfull and delightsome land."*

It was "fruitfull and delightsome" land, indeed, and it was not long before even the Jamestown settlers knew that there was much more of the same to the west, all the way to the Appalachians. And it was not too long after that before the descendants of those first settlers began to spy out the land across the mountains and see more of the same stretching all the way to the valley of the Mississippi River. And it was not too long after that before a land-hungry new nation began to cast a covetous gaze even farther west, all the way to the Pacific Ocean.

But just whose land was it that was being looked at with such yearning? The question still crops up, especially in the West, where many people feel beleaguered by federal land laws, wilderness withdrawals, and other government actions that prevent them from doing whatever they might want to do with lands they consider their own. So it was that ranchers, miners, county commissioners, and other like-minded folk rose up to protest President Clinton's designation of Grand Staircase-Escalante National Monument in Utah in September 1996. Some even went so far as to say that the President didn't have the right to designate the monument in the first place, because the land involved belonged to Utah, not the federal government. That the states are the only legitimate owners of the national lands is a fairly common belief in some parts of the West, and periodically you hear calls for the "return" of all national lands.

However, these lands can't be returned to the states because they never belonged to the states. By every legal measure, the national lands are owned by the federal government—which is to say, all Americans—even though it was a while before the government took possession.

First, of course, there were the original owners to deal with—the two million or so many-nationed, multilingual Native American people who once occupied what would become the United States. Within a few decades, treaties, warfare, devastating epidemics, and other European devices, acts, and accidents would essentially remove those original occupants from the Atlantic seaboard. The 1840s would see them eliminated almost entirely from the East, pushed across the Mississippi River to the Great Plains. And after another few decades of pressure from Spanish, Mexican, and American settlement and conquest, most of the Native Americans who remained after more than three centuries of steady attrition found themselves confined to reservations of great size and little value.

Long before this "final" disposition of the Indians, a few of the original 13 colonies thought they had settled the question of the land's ownership to their satisfaction. Massachusetts, Connecticut, North Carolina, South Carolina, Georgia, and Virginia had all received royal grants of land in America, whose northern and southern boundaries extended from the Atlantic to the Pacific, even when no one really knew just how far that might be. New York, though without a similar grant, still claimed a good part of the Ohio Valley because of a long-standing agreement with the Iroquois Indians.

None of these sea-to-shining-sea claims survived long after the original 13 colonies became states. For one thing, except for a big corner property that would become known as the Pacific Northwest and which remained in British hands, Spain controlled everything west of the Mississippi River (but would return control of the Louisiana Territory to France in 1802). For another, Maryland, Rhode Island, New Jersey, New Hampshire, Pennsylvania, and Delaware had never been given royal grants of land beyond their immediate borders, and these so-called landless colonies were jealous of their landed neighbors. When the Articles of Confederation were sent around to the colonies for ratification in 1778, thus beginning the process that ultimately would produce the United States, Maryland refused to sign unless the landed colonies turned all their western claims over to the central government.

In October 1780, the Continental Congress formally requested that the landed states relinquish all western land claims for the

purpose of creating a public domain. "Resolved," its declaration read, "that the unappropriated lands that may be ceded or relinquished to the United States, by any particular States, pursuant to the recommendation of Congress . . . shall be disposed of for the common benefit of the United States. . . ." One by one, each state ultimately acceded to the request (though it would take until 1802 before the last transfer was made).

In 1785, the Congress passed an ordinance that mandated the surveying of all the newly acquired national lands and established rules by which they might be settled in an orderly fashion. Surveyed lands were to be auctioned off as townships, each 36 square miles in size and divided into 36 numbered sections. In 1787, the Congress followed with another proclamation that established the procedures by which portions of the settled lands could be formed into territories and states. So it was that by 1803 most of the ceded land between the Appalachians and the

PAUL CHESLEY

JUST VISIBLE
THROUGH FOG,
*Minnesota's Grand
Portage National
Monument—
a reconstruction of
the trade headquarters
of a British fur-trading
outfit—stands behind
stockade walls on the
shores of Lake Superior.
Established in 1958,
Grand Portage is a
rarity in the national
lands system: an
instance in which Indian
Trust lands were given
back to the federal
government for
conservation and
historic preservation.*

Mississippi was either a territory, as were Indiana (including what later became Illinois) and Mississippi (including much of what later became Alabama), or a full-fledged state of the Union, as were Ohio, Kentucky, and Tennessee. Each of the new states had to forgo all claim to any land within their borders that had not already been auctioned off by the federal government.

As it turned out, there was not very much land left to forgo. From the beginning, land speculation flourished everywhere, rules were ignored or circumvented, and within just a couple of decades virtually all of the national land that had fallen to the federal government between the Appalachians and the Mississippi was gone. More than 373 million acres had been granted to soldiers and sailors in payment of military service, sold at bargain prices to individual settlers and speculators and organized land companies, or given to states to help finance education, wagon road construction, railroads, and other public projects.

NARROW-
LEAVED
CATTAILS

*rise to meet pine
branches in Blackwater
National Wildlife
Refuge (opposite).
The Maryland refuge,
one of 15 on the
Chesapeake Bay and
its tributaries, was
established in 1933 as
a sanctuary for eagles
and other migratory
bird species. Today, it
helps protect endan-
gered Delmarva fox
squirrels.*

But soon after the turn of the century there was suddenly more. In 1803, President Thomas Jefferson purchased the territory of Louisiana from France, and in 1819, Spain ceded Florida to the United States. In 1845, the nation annexed the Republic of Texas; however, the annexation agreement let Texas keep its land since the republic had been an independent nation. The following year, by treaty with Great Britain, the United States acquired most of the Pacific Northwest. In 1848, after the conclusion of the Mexican War, came California and most of the Southwest, and, with the Gadsden Purchase of 1853, came the rest of the Southwest. Finally, Alaska was purchased from Russia in 1867.

Over a period of less than 70 years, then, the national patrimony of land was enlarged by more than 1.6 billion acres between the Mississippi River and the Pacific Coast, including Alaska. All but the 171 million acres of Texas was owned by the public—federal land, national land. Today, only about 630 million acres of national lands are left.

SOME OF THE LAND—about 90 million acres—went to various Indian peoples as tribal land, trust land, or land administered by the Bureau of Indian Affairs on their behalf. A little over 4.5 million acres ended up under the jurisdiction of the Bureau of Reclamation, an Interior Department agency devoted to the building of federal dams and irrigation projects. Another 25 million acres were taken up in various kinds of military installations. The rest of the roughly 605 million acres that vanished from the national lands bank between the beginning of the 19th century and the first years of the 20th century was simply disposed of with stunning profligacy.

It was all done to settle and make prosperous the newly acquired western territories. "The American claim is by right of our manifest destiny to overspread and to possess the whole of the continent which Providence has given us," wrote journalist John Louis O'Sullivan in 1845. "It is a right such as that of the tree to the space of air and earth suitable for the full expansion of its principle and destiny of growth."

So the government was generous, if often careless in its benevolence. To railroads such as the Union Pacific, Central Pacific, and Southern Pacific went some 130 million acres of the national lands to help finance the construction of railroad systems from the Mississippi River to the Pacific Coast. To the states went about 150 million acres, some through the Swamp Lands Act of

1850 or various direct grants for public construction projects; much acreage was given away under the stipulations of the Morrill Land Grant Act of 1862, designed to help the western states establish agricultural colleges. In addition, Alaska got a special grant of 104 million acres to provide the territory with an economic base when it became a state in 1959. Title to another 250 million acres of national land passed to farmers and ranchers who filed and "proved up" the land under the provisions of the Homestead Act of 1862 and other such laws. And, while the General Mining Law of 1872 did not dispose of a great deal of land, it gave away hundreds of billions of dollars in treasure that lay beneath the national lands by charging mining companies not a dime in royalties.

DAVID MUENCH

More than 700 million acres gone. Even at the height of this frenzied giveaway there were those who decried it, especially the grants to the railroads. "While fighting to retain eleven refractory states," one critic wrote in the middle of the Civil War, "the nation permits itself to be cozened out of territory sufficient to form twelve new republics."

Not many were listening. Everyone was too busy building railroads and advertising their railroad grant lands for sale, bringing in swarms of people from all points of the country and the world. They were exterminating millions of American bison to feed the railroad-builders and send meat, hides, and bones to eastern markets. They were driving cattle up from Texas and other southern points to be fattened on the protein-rich grasses of the High Plains, or filling the mountain meadows with sheep, until livestock reduced many of the West's grasslands to barrens wrecked by erosion.

People were plowing and planting in a land that had too little water to support their dreams. Between 1862 and 1880 fewer than half of those who had filed claims under the Homestead Act lasted long enough to acquire final title to their land, and those who remained sent up a cry for irrigation projects that ultimately would dam most of the wild rivers of the West. People were cutting down and hauling out Douglas fir and western red cedar from the national lands of the Pacific Northwest, redwood in northern California, and ponderosa pine, yellow pine and lodgepole pine in the Rockies—until at one point the federal government was advised to sell the forest lands while there were still any trees left. And people were digging up gold and silver and copper everywhere they could find it in a frenzy that one reporter of the 1860s compared to war: "It was," he wrote, "as if a wondrous battle raged, in which the combatants were men and earth."

THE BATTLE IS ONE we don't like to think about much, preferring the myth of the West as a big, beautiful stage on which mountain men, pioneering families, cowboys, grizzled prospectors, and brave but hopelessly outnumbered Indians played out a great folktale. Historian Bernard DeVoto was closer to the mark when he called the West the "Plundered Province." But even as the plunder began, another kind of sensibility was developing. In the end, this too would become part of the western story, and its most important legacy would be the preserved remnants of beauty and life in the 630 million acres of the national lands system.

Like all great social movements, what came to be called conservation—and later, environmentalism—was driven in large part by the ideas and leadership of a few inspired individuals. In 1864, for instance, a Vermont visionary by the name of George Perkins Marsh wrote *Man and Nature*. The book looked back on all the ruined civilizations of the past, determined that they fell because they abused the environment, and predicted that the United States was in grave danger of doing the same—particularly if it continued to cut its forests with such abandon. "It is certain," he wrote, "that a desolation, like that which has overwhelmed many once beautiful and fertile regions of Europe, awaits an important part of the territory of the United States. . . unless prompt measures are taken to check the action of destructive causes already in operation."

Marsh's wisdom, while not universally acknowledged or acclaimed, did not exactly fall upon deaf ears. Even then, there were some, in and out of government, who suspected that the freewheeling days of the land's exploitation might be drawing to a close. Explorer and scientist John Wesley Powell, who helped create the U.S. Geological Survey, for example, was telling Congress in the 1870s that the aridity of most of the West made the Homestead Act—as well as traditional farming and ranching methods—inappropriate west of the 100th meridian.

In the late 1880s, nature itself stepped in to make the point. Heavy rains in the Appalachians poured off the timber-stripped hills straight into the rivers, swelling them well over flood stage and sending them boiling into towns and cities, including the streets of Pittsburgh. Up in Johnstown, Pennsylvania, in 1889, rain caused so much water to spill into a local reservoir that its badly maintained dam burst and more than 2,000 people were killed by a 40-foot wall of water that raged through the town.

That kind of evidence was hard to miss, and in 1891 President Benjamin Harrison's Interior Secretary, John W. Noble, inserted a rider in a public lands bill that permitted the President to "set apart and reserve, in any State or Territory. . .any part of the public lands wholly or in part covered with timber or undergrowth . . .as public reservations." Congress passed the public lands bill without paying too much attention to the rider. As a result, within a few months President Harrison had put 13 million acres of forests off-limits to logging.

The forest reserves were an idea whose time had come, certainly in the opinion of a young forester by the name of Gifford Pinchot, a man of good Connecticut stock and great ambition. Pinchot, who was later governor of Pennsylvania, served on a presidential forestry commission in 1896 and was among those who recommended to President Grover Cleveland that even more forest reserves should be made. Cleveland agreed, but insisted that Congress give him some sort of management plan.

Pinchot helped write legislation to that effect, and on June 4, 1897, the Forest Organic Act was passed. The forest reserves were meant to "improve and protect the forest," the act declared, ". . . for the purpose of securing favorable conditions of water flow, and to furnish a continuous supply of timber for the use and necessities of the people of the United States." By now, some 40 million acres of forest had been set aside, and Cleveland appointed Pinchot to head up the Department of Agriculture's Division of Forestry, which monitored the reserves.

However, the General Land Office of the Interior Department actually managed the reserves, while the role of the Department of Agriculture was merely advisory. Pinchot lobbied to have administration of the forests transferred *(Continued on page 80)*

(Continued on page 80)

FOLLOWING PAGES: *Waves of mist roll over the green and gold hills of Great Smoky Mountains National Park, a national lands unit in the southern Appalachian Mountains. The combined efforts of Tennessee, North Carolina, and John D. Rockefeller, Jr.—who donated five million dollars in honor of his mother—helped to purchase the lands to establish the park in 1934. Today it is the most heavily visited park in the National Park System.*

MARC MUENCH

MOTTLED WHITE TRUNKS *of birch trees punctuate the autumn color in the woods of Michigan's Pictured Rocks National Lakeshore, which runs 40 miles along the southeastern edge of*

CARR CLIFTON/MINDEN PICTURES

Lake Superior. Nearly a century after the designation of Yellowstone as America's first national park, the new idea of national lakeshores emerged. Pictured Rocks, established in 1966, was the first of four.

HIGH PLAINS STORM
broods over an isolated house on BLM lands near Medicine Bow, Wyoming. Those who tried to stake their claim in plains country were among the many thousands who saw the "leftover lands" west of the Missouri River as a dream of opportunity —a dream that often was dashed by an inhospitable climate.

PAUL CHESLEY

CARR CLIFTON/MINDEN PICTURES

HAUNTING, LIFE-SIZE FIGURES
painted in red ocher (opposite) decorate the Great
Gallery, one of many sites of prehistoric art that dot
Utah's Canyonlands National Park, established in
1964. Horseshoe Canyon, where the Great Gallery
is located, was added to the park in 1971 specifically
to protect these ancient drawings, made by a hunter-
gatherer culture dating from 1700 B.C. to A.D. 500
The ruins of pueblo walls (below) cast shadows in
the sun in Mesa Verde National Park, Colorado.
Established by President Theodore Roosevelt in
1906, Mesa Verde is the only national park
dedicated entirely to the preservation of man-made
works, chiefly those of the ancestral Puebloans who
lived in the region from about A.D. 500 to 1270.
With more than 4,000 prehistoric sites, Mesa Verde
has one of the most complete existing records of the
ancestral Puebloan culture.

PAUL CHESLEY

COILED INTO THE RED-ROCK HEART *of the Colorado Plateau on BLM land in Utah, the*
Dirty Devil River makes its way to Lake Powell. The river got its name after John Wesley Powell and his

PAUL CHESLEY

men declared, "It stinks like a dirty devil." The intricate canyons the river has incised in the plateau are the subject of heated controversy in the ongoing debate over BLM wilderness preservation in Utah.

**DOMINATING
THE MOUNTAINSCAPE,**
*12,945-foot Banner Peak in the Ansel
Adams Wilderness soars above Thousand
Island Lake in California's Sierra Nevada.
Named in honor of the renowned nature
photographer and devoted conservationist,
the wilderness in both Inyo and Sierra
National Forests encompasses 231,066
acres of peaks, fell-fields, glacial lakes, and
high-elevation forests.*

from Interior to Agriculture, and in 1905 he succeeded in persuading President Theodore Roosevelt to make the switch. Roosevelt also established the U.S. Forest Service and made Pinchot the nation's first chief forester. Before he left office, Roosevelt swung the big stick of presidential power again to create another 86 million acres of reserves. These, like those made by Harrison and Cleveland, were all in the West, since by then nearly every acre of forestland in the East was in private hands. Passage of the Weeks Act in 1911 and the Clarke-McNary Act in 1924 rectified that problem, authorizing the purchase of private forestland by the Forest Service. The acts also helped bring the system up to its present level of 191 million acres (including the 4.2 million acres of national grasslands) by adding new forests in many eastern states, from Florida to New Hampshire.

EVEN BEFORE ROOSEVELT and Pinchot established the National Forest System, the National Park System was well under way. Indeed, the idea for national parks predated that of the national forests by more than 50 years and differed from it in one important aspect. Under Pinchot and his successors, the national forests were considered essential to the economic health of the nation. Forest cover protected watersheds, assuring a supply of clean drinking water and preventing the kind of floods that had devastated so much of the Appalachian region in the 1880s. Forests also provided timber for commercial use, and, while conservationists have found much to complain about in the way the Forest Service has promoted logging as the dominant use of most of the forests since World War II, timber production remains an important function of these lands.

National parks, by contrast, at first were not seen to have much practical value. Indeed, the very fact that such areas generally contained nothing that anybody wanted for commercial purposes was one of the best arguments park promoters had in their efforts to persuade Congress to establish them in the first place. In the absence of practical value, the great motivators for creating national parks were their beauty and uniqueness and the sense of wonder they inspired. Certainly these attributes fueled the enthusiasm of artist George Catlin. In 1832, after spending some time painting Indians in the High Plains country of Dakota Territory, Catlin urged that much of the land, complete with its Indians, be set aside as "A *nation's Park*, containing man and beast, in all the wild and freshness of their nature's beauty!" Catlin's idea was far ahead of its time, but 32 years later its echo was heard when the federal government in 1864 gave the state of California the region of the Yosemite Valley and a grove of Big Trees— *Sequoiadendron giganteum*—to be managed as state parks "for public use, resort, and recreation." The government also ordered that their wonders were to be maintained as "inalienable." In other words, Yosemite and the Big Trees were to be preserved in their natural state or the grant would be rendered invalid.

Preservation was the goal of the first true national park, too, one that remained in federal ownership. "The intelligent American," government explorer Ferdinand Vandiveer Hayden wrote after visiting the upper Yellowstone River in 1871, "will one day point on the map to this remarkable district with the conscious pride that it has not its parallel on the face of the globe." Pride was made manifest in 1872, when Congress established the 2.2-million-acre Yellowstone National Park "dedicated and set apart as a public park or pleasuring-ground for the benefit and enjoyment of the people." Further, the Secretary of the Interior was instructed to so manage the park that its natural wonders and wildlife were to be preserved "in their natural condition."

In 1890, another visionary went into action. John Muir, a self-taught naturalist who would help found the Sierra Club in 1892 and who knew the Sierra Nevada, especially the Yosemite Valley, better than anyone in the United States, prodded Congress until it established Sequoia and Big Trees National Parks (the Big Trees portion would later be folded into Sequoia) and designated the mountain meadows and peaks surrounding the Yosemite Valley as Yosemite National Park. Meanwhile, since 1864, the state of California had done a slipshod job of meeting its obligation to keep the Yosemite Valley itself uncorrupted. Eventually, at Muir's urging, the valley was returned to the federal government and joined to Yosemite National Park in 1905.

By 1916, with a total of 14 national parks and 21 national monuments, the National Park System had grown big enough to require some centralized administration. The U.S. Army had served that purpose in Yellowstone and many of the parks for years, though imperfectly, but the monuments were left in the hands of whatever agency had controlled the land out of which the monuments were carved. A National Park Service was needed, reformers insisted, an agency with powers similar to those of the U.S. Forest Service. Moreover, the parks needed legislation that would codify their purpose and coordinate their management policies. Congress complied, passing the National Park Service Act of 1916, which declared it the purpose of the national parks

FIERY STREAMS

of molten lava
pouring into cold
Pacific surf create
clouds of steam on
the shores of Hawaii
Volcanoes National
Park. Located on the
south coast of the Big
Island of Hawaii, the
park is one of only
two national parks
in the state. Its active
volcanism—evidence
of a hot spot under
the Pacific plate—
is a living lesson
in the planet's
geological dynamism.

to "conserve the scenery and the natural and historic objects and the wildlife therein and to provide for the enjoyment of the same in such manner and by such means as will leave them unimpaired for the enjoyment of future generations." As the National Park System grew, so did the American population, and eventually the administrative focus of the National Park Service evolved. While the Service's earliest challenge had been to entice people into the parks so as to foster appreciation and support in the general public, the challenge today is to figure out how to let hundreds of millions of visitors continue to experience the parks every year without "loving them to death," in the favorite phrase of conservationists.

I F THE NATIONAL PARK SYSTEM was the child of wonder, the National Wildlife Refuge System was the child of loss. The careless extermination of millions of bison in the 1860s and 1870s gave it birth. So did the loss of the passenger pigeons that once darkened the skies from Canada to Florida, slaughtered by market hunters and deprived of habitat by development. So did the assault on waterfowl by sportsmen and commercial hunters alike, particularly the near-annihilation of egrets, whose gleaming white feathers were valued in the decoration of women's hats. So did the crashing populations of heath hens, Labrador ducks, Carolina parakeets,

great auks, eastern panthers, all through hunting or destruction of their habitats, or both.

By the beginning of the 20th century, the United States seemed in danger of eliminating dozens of wild species valued for their beauty, their singularity, or their appeal as prey for the enjoyment of hunters. Led by sportsman George Bird Grinnell, editor of *Forest and Stream* and organizer of the first version of an Audubon Society, along with scientists in the American Ornithologists Union and people who simply loved wild creatures, a wildlife preservation movement evolved whose ultimate contribution was the creation of the National Wildlife Refuge System. Most of the pieces from which the refuge system was assembled were national lands.

Beginning with Pelican Island in Florida, which Theodore Roosevelt designated a "federal bird reservation" in 1903, the national refuge system grew in fits and starts. Responsibility for its administration was first given to the Bureau of Biological Survey, an agency of the Department of Agriculture. (In 1939, the Biological Survey would be taken out of the Department of Agriculture and put into Interior. In 1940, it would be made part of the newly created Fish and Wildlife Service.) Passage of the Duck Stamp Act in 1934, authorizing the use of proceeds from bird-hunting licenses to buy land for the purpose of creating refuges, gave the conservation-minded administration of President Franklin D. Roosevelt the means to buy private land in the East to enlarge the system.

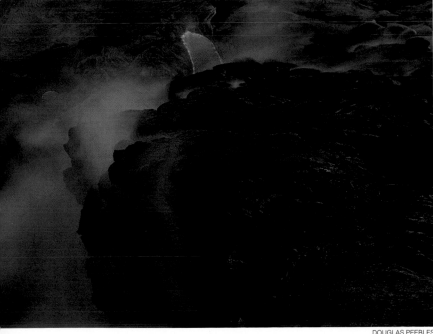

DOUGLAS PEEBLES

DAVID MUENCH

STILL, EVEN UNDER an ambitious purchase program initiated by Survey chief J.N. "Ding" Darling (a popular editorial cartoonist by trade), the refuge system had grown to only 17.6 million acres by 1939. Not until passage of the Alaska National Interest Lands Conservation Act of 1980—more simply known as the Alaska Lands Act—did the system achieve the respectable dimensions of today, with more than 500 individual refuges adding up to more than 92 million acres. Unlike the other three segments of the national lands system, the refuge system did not get its own management directive from Congress—an "organic act"—until passage of the National Wildlife Refuge System Improvement Act in the fall of 1997. Until then, it was administered by regulations developed within the USFWS that often hampered what conservationists considered the only truly "compatible" use of the refuges: the protection and preservation of wildlife and its habitat.

The largest portion of the national lands system, the 264 million acres now administered by the Bureau of Land Management in most of the western states, also was without its own "organic" act for many years, until 1976. In 1934 the Taylor Grazing Act placed about 140 million acres under the supervision of the Division of Grazing (later renamed the Grazing Service) in an attempt to control overgrazing and prevent erosion and other environmental degradation. The rest remained in the control of the Interior Department's General Land Office. In 1946 the Grazing Service and the General Land Office were both abolished and their responsibilities placed in the hands of the newly created BLM. But it was another 30 years before passage of the Federal Land Policy and Management Act attempted to bring direction to the management of these lands. Nevertheless, they continued to be regarded by almost everyone in government as worthless for much of anything but the extraction of minerals or the feeding of cattle and sheep.

By now, however, the BLM is beginning to appreciate that these lands—and indeed, all of the national lands system—embrace a dwindling and priceless resource of habitat diversity, landscape beauty, and wildlife. Even John Smith, were he around to visit the Chesapeake Bay today, might reconsider his wish to see the surrounding land "fully manured and inhabited by industrious people." As naturalist Henry David Thoreau wrote almost a century and a half ago: "In Wildness is the preservation of the World....A town is saved, not more by the righteous men in it than by the woods and swamps that surround it."

TUCKED INTO AN OPENING *in a massive wall of red sandstone (opposite), an ancient pueblo called the White House Ruin in Arizona's Canyon de Chelly National Monument attests to the antiquity of the human presence in the desert Southwest.*

FOLLOWING PAGES: *Navajo shepherds tend their flock on the floor of Canyon de Chelly. When the canyon was made a national monument in 1931, the Navajo retained ownership, but agreed to let the National Park Service manage public access.*

PAUL CHESLEY

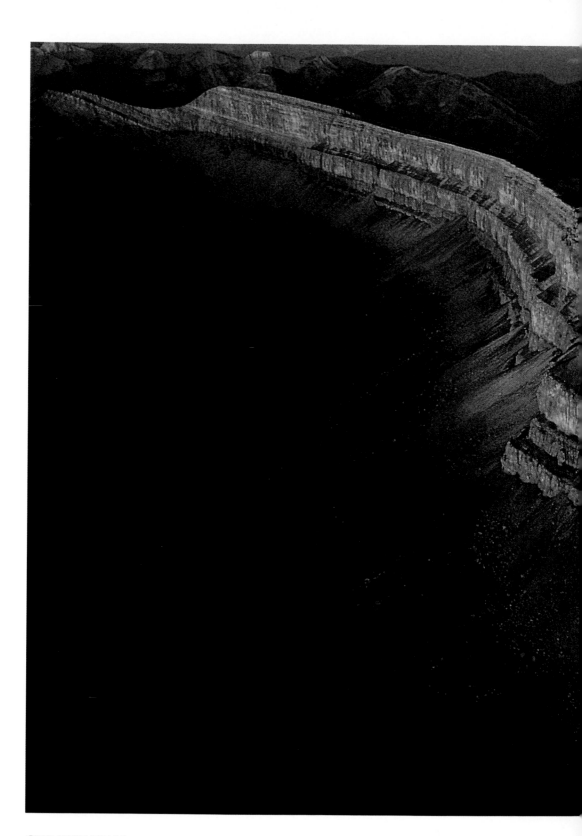

CHINESE WALL, *a stratified limestone escarpment some 12 miles long, glints in the sun in the Bob Marshall Wilderness of Montana's Flathead and Lewis and Clark National Forests. Marshall was*

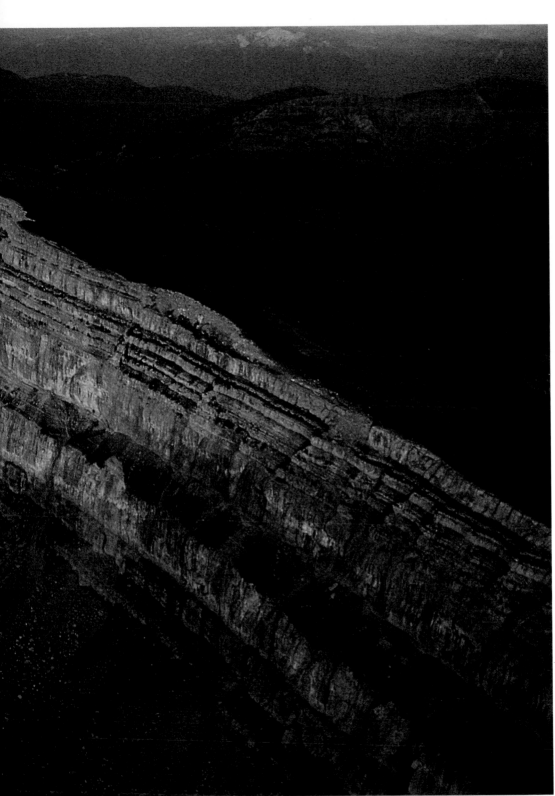

PAUL CHESLEY

an inspired Forest Service official who, in the 1930s, conceived and actively promoted the idea that the country should establish a national wilderness preservation system.

BLACK ROCK DESERT
stretches to a cloudy horizon on BLM
lands northwest of the Humboldt River
in Nevada. Parched and barren, the desert
was not a regular route for wagon-train
pioneers, but in the 1840s and 1850s,
some gold seekers attempted to use it as
a shortcut to Oregon and California.

JAMES P. BLAIR

SHALLOW WATER IN A TIDAL POOL *reflects rounded stones scattered along a segment of Washington's Olympic National Park. The 57-mile-long ocean strip was described by the late Supreme*

DAVID MUENCH

Court Justice William O. Douglas—a passionate conservationist—as "the one remaining piece of thoroughly primitive beach on the whole coastline of the United States....It is wild, raw, beautiful."

The Safety Valve

AS STRENUOUS CHALLENGE
OR CONTEMPLATIVE RETREAT,
THE PARKS AND OTHER UNITS OF THE
NATIONAL LANDS OFFER WELCOME RESPITE
FROM THE WORLD, A SAFETY VALVE
FOR BODY AND SPIRIT.

· ·

ABUNDANT CHOICE: *Rest and recreation are readily available on the national lands, from sunning on a sandy beach in Virgin Islands National Park (opposite) to scrambling up an ice wall in San Juan National Forest, Colorado (above).*

TOM BEAN (OPPOSITE); PAUL CHESLEY (ABOVE)

BUCKING THE WAVES
on the Colorado River through the Grand Canyon, today's river runners thrill to the challenge much as did explorer John Wesley Powell and his men when they tried it in 1869. The double-ended dories Powell used were similar to the craft worked here by river guide Jeff Schloss.

TOM BEAN

"IN WILD COUNTRY the sky comes down clear to the ground," read some 1970s promotional copy for the Sierra Club. "Not just to the tops of buildings. There are no fences around flowers, no cages for birds. And you can walk on the grass. Inner city kids can't get over it....it changes forever their way of looking at things." The Sierra Club had begun a program that brought disadvantaged city children into the national parks and national forests of the Sierra Nevada as a way of introducing them to a world they would otherwise have known only as images on television. Today there are similar programs all over the country, and most of the time the effect is the same: The kids are beatified, at least for a moment, by the discovery of wildness they find in the national lands. Their senses are alive—perhaps for the first time—to the sights, sounds, smells, and sheer physical presence of nature in the raw.

Sometimes you don't have to go all the way to the mountains to find it. The sky comes down clear to the ground in Gateway National Recreation Area in New York, for example, where every year some 15,000 young people are introduced to nature by the National Park Service through various school programs. At Jamaica Bay Wildlife Refuge, children from Harlem, the Bronx, and other areas of New York City learn to identify and watch for some of the more than 300 bird species that have been recorded at the site, dip their hands in the waters of the bay, and look for insects and shells, while behind them rise the towers of Brooklyn, and the skies above John F. Kennedy International Airport fill with the screams of jetliners.

Other children enjoy similar nature study programs at Gateway units such as Sandy Hook, off the coast of New Jersey, where holly forests and long stretches of beach can be found at the sky's edge, or Great Kills Park on Staten Island, home to migrating flocks of monarch butterflies. More youngsters take part in overnight camping adventures at the Jamaica Bay unit's Floyd Bennett Field, and others learn how to garden in nearby plots.

"Believe it or not," Manny Strumpf, Park Service spokesman for Gateway, told me, "some of these kids have never even known where tomatoes come from, much less anything about nature in general. The experience can transform them." When the children return to the concrete and asphalt of the city, the hope is that they will carry with them a lasting memory of the largeness and life they found at Gateway and other urban parks.

All of us, no matter how insulated from the worst aspects of our troubled society, need a connection to the wild—passage into what Wallace Stegner called "the geography of hope." While social scientists and other academics tend to use the word "recreation" to describe everything from television viewing to sandlot baseball, if you break it down into its component parts, its deepest meaning is precisely revealed: re-creation. To be made again.

Every year, tens of millions of Americans seek that renewal. When measured against the billions of dollars that all the timber, grazing land, oil, gas, coal, gold, silver, copper, and other material treasures the national lands give us annually, recreation might be considered worthless in the material sense. In fact, however, park entrance fees and fees for various types of recreation on the national lands bring in significant income. The BLM estimates that in 1996 its recreation fees earned the agency nearly one million dollars, while in that same year the total expenditures by visitors for food, supplies, gas, and other ancillary expenses accounted for more than 735 million dollars. For its part, the Forest Service estimates that by the year 2000, recreation in the national forests will bring in 110.7 billion dollars of revenue annually, as opposed to 3.5 billion dollars from timber contracts.

THESE ARE NOT PALTRY NUMBERS, but I'm not sure anyone can ever put a fixed price on what recreation actually provides. How do you measure the worth of emotional and spiritual restoration? Someone sitting on the top of a mountain in Prescott National Forest, watching a golden eagle slowly spiral up a column of rising air until it is lost in the glare of the sun could not put a price on the experience. Neither could some hardy soul using only hands and feet to "free climb" up the sheer face of a 500-foot cliff in Yosemite National Park. Someone casting a dry fly into a dark and promising hole on the Madison River in Montana's Gallatin National Forest, or carrying a bow and arrow and following the track of a ten-point buck in New Hampshire's White Mountain National Forest would be hard-pressed to put a dollar figure on the challenge of his pursuit.

Whether one is frantically gripping the edge of a rubber raft while it bounces through a howling rapid on the Wild and Scenic Salmon River, or peering through the windshield of the car, while bison, bighorn sheep, and sometimes wolves and grizzlies prowl the landscape of Yellowstone National Park, the heart's excitement

SHROUDED
IN FOG,
*the old lighthouse at
Sandy Hook in New
Jersey rises above a
woodland in Gateway
National Recreation
Area. A complex of
islands, marshes,
woods, and ocean
beach in portions of
Long Island, Staten
Island, and New Jersey,
Gateway mixes history
and nature in a
recreational blend
experienced by as
many as 15,000
youngsters each year.*

is beyond measure. And where's the price tag when a small girl from Harlem stands surrounded by a bright swarm of monarch butterflies at Great Kills Park on Staten Island? Such a moment is worth nothing—and everything.

As a recreational resource, then, the national lands themselves are priceless. Americans seem to know that, even if they don't always know where the lands came from or much about who manages them for what reason. They demonstrate their realization by simply showing up, in numbers that are staggering: In 1996, the National Forest System recorded 859 million recreation visits, the National Park System 172 million (not including visits to national battlefields and other non-natural sites), the BLM lands 58.9 million, and the National Wildlife Refuge System 29.5 million. That

MARC MUENCH

amounts to more than 1.1 billion times that Americans exercised their right to enjoy their own land in 1996, a figure that logic suggests is going to continue to increase in the years ahead.

How Americans enjoy the lands is as various as the lands themselves, for the national lands offer just about every definition of fun likely to appeal to a human being at any given moment. In any national park, national monument, or national recreation area you can fish anywhere there are enough fish to make it worth your while. Every summer, as you drive into Yellowstone National Park from Livingston, Montana, for example, fly fishermen and -women adorn nearly every bend of the Yellowstone River for as far as the eye can see, acting out the graceful, Zen-like rituals of their sport. You can hunt as well as fish in the few national preserves in the lower forty-eight and all of the big preserves in Alaska, such as Wrangell-St. Elias National Park and Preserve. In most of the West, however, hunting is confined to national forests or BLM lands. The Forest Service says that its lands enjoyed more than 19 million visits by hunters in 1996, and although the BLM does not separate hunters from fishermen in its own statistics, the agency's records show 10.6 million hunting and fishing visits for the year. Interestingly, even though sport hunters were vocal and active in supporting the growth of the National Wildlife Refuge System, only 1.5 million hunters took advantage of the refuges in 1996.

Most of those who practice hunting maintain that when it is pursued with a decent respect for the life of the animal, it brings them closer to an understanding of the complexities and beauty of the natural world than any other form of recreation. Some non-hunters tend to object to the dangers that hunting holds for those, like themselves, who happen to walk in harm's way in the woods in the wrong season. It is an old argument, and no closer to being set-tled on the national lands than anywhere else in the country.

SOME VISITORS to the national lands prefer recreation as mind-altering exhilaration. Mountain climbing on Mount McKinley in Denali National Park and Preserve in Alaska or white-water kayaking down the New River in West Virginia are but two activities and venues that attract visitors to the nation's lands. According to a Forest Service report on winter sports, "Nearly 60 percent of all downhill skiing in the United States occurs on the national forests. Thirty-one million lift tickets were sold at ski resorts on national forests during the 1995-1996 winter season." The impact of all those national forest ski lifts and lift-ticket holders is considerable. "A look at the amount of lodging, residential, and retail development snaking through the valleys beneath the ski slopes west of Denver," one skiing journalist has written, "is a quick education in the meaning of the term 'cumulative impacts' from ski-area development." Indeed, skiing accounts for the great bulk of the roughly 20 million winter-sports visitors to the national forests every year. Proposed expansions and plans for entirely new ski areas are popping up from San Bernardino National Forest in California to San Juan National Forest in Colorado.

In what has come to characterize the atmosphere surrounding any proposed development on any national lands, some of these ski areas are vehemently opposed by environmentalists. Other forms of national lands recreation have inspired equally energetic opposition—or at least some legitimate worry. The BLM's "Back Country Byways" program, for example, has tremendous appeal. Numerous old roads, some of them paved, others scarcely more than ancient wagon tracks or single-track dirt trails, curl through the BLM lands of the West, through mountain passes and over mesa tops, up narrow, rock-walled canyons, in and out of old mining camps and other historic sites, past wonderful geologic formations and other scenic marvels.

Conservation organizations like the Wilderness Society and the Southern Utah Wilderness Alliance have helped to identify such roads as a means of getting a look at some of the wilderness that needs protecting. From the Black Rock Desert of Nevada to the Kaiparowits Plateau of southern Utah, these roads provide a singularly delightful way of learning just what wonders the BLM lands hold. That opportunity is what the agency had in mind when it began the Back Country Byways program in 1990. "We always like to see more people use BLM land," a BLM spokesman said at the time. "It belongs to them, after all. And we're really pleased with the Back Country Byways idea—it will give people a chance to see what they've got here."

Sixty roads are being promoted by the BLM as part of the program, including 51 miles of dirt-and-gravel along Big Sheep Creek in Montana and a 47-mile deeply rutted stretch into the Hualapai Mountains of Arizona. Though some signs have been put up to keep people from getting lost, almost no road improvements will be made on these byways, and most require four-wheel-drive vehicles for safe traveling. In fact, each road is designated by its surface and the type of vehicle required, and the BLM closes some roads in winter or during rainy seasons, so as to keep vehicles from making deeper ruts. Drivers are also asked not to attempt shortcuts by crossing unroaded country, not to drive up streambeds, and otherwise to proceed in an intelligent and courteous manner: No littering. No vandalism.

Like most federal land-managing agencies, however, the BLM is understaffed and must rely on the cooperation of the people using the roads to keep them from being abused. Thus, as the popularity of the byways program grows, so does the potential for damage to the surrounding landscape. Now, although I do enjoy crawling along the BLM byways, I confess that I don't have much empathy for most other off-road fun—the kind of glee provided by dirt bikes, dune buggies, all-terrain vehicles (ATVs), and snowmobiles. As I watch swarms of dirt bikers race across the Mojave Desert, I am all too aware that they are tearing (Continued on page 114)

FOLLOWING PAGES: *While feeding intently, a velvet-antlered moose looks up from a meal in Alaska's Kenai National Wildlife Refuge. Moose, like caribou, can be game for both sport and subsistence hunting in Alaska, and the millions of acres of refuges, preserves, and national forests in the state provide essential habitat to maintain populations of these animals.*

MICHIO HOSHINO/MINDEN PICTURES

TESTING THE RUNS *of Aspen Mountain in Colorado's White River National Forest, skiers appear oblivious to an ominous sky. Fun, the U.S. Forest Service has learned, is considerably more profitable than*

PAUL CHESLEY

timber cutting. By the year 2000, the agency expects forestlands to generate 110.7 billion dollars every year from recreation (including hunting and fishing) and only 3.5 billion dollars from logging.

CANOEIST'S PARADISE
greets paddlers as they enter Minnesota's
Boundary Waters Canoe Area Wilderness
in Superior National Forest, one of several
designated wilderness areas established
directly by the Wilderness Act of 1964.
To maintain its wilderness character, about
three-quarters of Boundary Waters is
off-limits to motorized boating.

PAUL CHESLEY

PLUMES OF SAND *spill from the wheel of a reproduction 1856 handcart in a modern reenactment, on BLM lands, that pays tribute to 19th-century Mormon "handcart" pioneers. Between 1856 and 1860,*

PAUL CHESLEY

2,900 Mormons dragged their worldly goods nearly 1,400 miles from the Missouri River to Utah's Great Salt Lake. In 1856, two parties of these pioneers were trapped in early snows and more than 200 people died.

DWARFED BY ITS ENORMITY,
four visitors to Arizona's Grand Canyon
National Park take in the spectacular view
from the popular South Rim. In 1996,
4.5 million people visited the park, arriving
from all over the country and the world.

TOM BEAN

up the soil and filling the air with reverberation and dust. In Cooke City, Montana, in winter, as I watch snowmobilers buzz up and down the main street, then career off into Yellowstone National Park on groomed snow-covered roads, I worry about the mule deer and elk and other creatures already stressed by winter. In both desert and snow, I can't help but wonder how close to nature you really get when you put so much horsepower and so many decibels between yourself and the rest of creation.

MORE GENTLE PURSUITS have much to recommend them. In the national forests alone, where there are more than 133,000 miles of hiking trails, including nearly 6,000 miles of the National Scenic Trails System, at least 30 million hikes take place every year. The BLM does not keep figures in its Public Land Statistics on the number of miles of trails its lands hold, but 28 million people engaged in what the agency calls "trail activities" in 1996. The National Wildlife Refuge System, for its part, had 5.4 million trail visits that year. The national parks, of course, are laced by thousands of trails on which virtually everyone who visits a park ends up walking at one time or another.

All of this activity suggests that millions of Americans are seeking renewal by getting as close to the land as their feet will take them. And many of those same millions are letting their feet do the walking in what may be the single most important thing the national lands can offer the poor, addled human spirit in the way of recreation: wilderness, designated wilderness, federal wilderness, American wilderness. No other nation on earth has anything to compare with the National Wilderness Preservation System of the United States. Like jazz and the Bill of Rights—like the national lands themselves—officially classified wilderness is a uniquely American idea, found only on these lands.

Recently, considerable discussion has arisen over the question of just how "wild" designated wilderness truly is, given that human beings have been in and on the land ever since the first peoples emigrated here from Siberia, perhaps 20,000 years ago. As they moved down the continent, splitting up into language groups, and splitting up again into nations called tribes, they set fires to create better hunting grounds. They grafted one plant species onto another to engineer something they could cultivate and eat. They carved hunting and trading trails through wilderness or over plains. They built irrigation works and huge burial mounds, and erected whole cities made of earth. They did any number of things that to one degree or another altered the land in measurable ways.

That being the case, this argument goes, designating certain pieces of landscape worthy of protection because they contain a relic of "primeval" America is illogical at best. What we are protecting is not a place but an idea.

As it happens, the Wilderness Act of 1964 doesn't say anything about "primeval" or even "pristine." What it does say is this: "A wilderness, in contrast with those areas where man and his own works dominate the landscape, is hereby recognized as an area where the earth and its community of life are untrammeled by man, where man himself is a visitor who does not remain...." That seems good enough for most of those who think that such areas, however marked or traversed or otherwise touched by human beings they might have been over the past several millennia, still are as close to the truly wild as most people are ever likely to get. As Wallace Stegner wrote, "We simply need that wild country available to us, even if we never do more than drive to its edge and look in. For it can be a means of reassuring ourselves of our sanity as creatures...."

I can attest that sanity is the point. Though I reside now in a small western town surrounded by mountains, I spent 37 years of my life in large cities, walled off from all but the most cursory connection to the natural world. True, San Francisco and Oakland in California did have San Francisco Bay, but even when I lived there in the 1960s and 1970s, the Bay was threatened by development. Only a grassroots citizens' movement kept its shores from being filled in and built upon. New York City has Central Park, but that is an entirely manufactured place. Washington, D.C., where I lived for nearly 16 years, has big old white oaks and maples lining the streets and ornamenting the city's squares and circles, but all were planted by humans long ago and have a regimental character; only the 1,754 acres of Rock Creek Park hold at least a suggestion of wildness.

But even in my big-city days, my work as a writer enabled me to hop airplanes to someplace wild fairly often. The sudden feeling of freedom and anticipatory excitement that came over me when I stepped out of the airport in Salt Lake City, got into a rental car, and headed for the canyon country of southern Utah was as real as it is indescribable. Every single time I did so—not every now and then, but every single time—whether heading for the Escalante River or pointing myself toward

PERCHED ON *a spit of sand, two campers fish the twilight waters of Florida Bay at the southern tip of Everglades National Park. Though the park is only minutes away from the long conurbation of Florida's southeast coast, 1.2 million acres of Everglades is designated wilderness. Thousands of people every year come to experience its mix of wetland habitat and species, from mangrove swamps to saw-grass plains, alligators to wood storks.*

the backcountry Rockies or the California desert or the Everglades or any other place that holds a wilderness treasure, I felt as if I were coming home.

I WAS COMING HOME, and so are those city kids getting their first sight—courtesy of the National Park Service—of a living wild creature, or a holly forest, or a seascape or valley or marshland. So are other people one would not ordinarily expect to see traipsing around in wilderness areas—elderly people, or disabled folks for example. But such pilgrims do visit federal lands, and they are doing so in increasing numbers, thanks to their own gumption and to organizations like Wilderness Inquiry, based in Minneapolis, Minnesota; Breckenridge Outdoor Education Center, located near Denver, Colorado; or the Cooperative Wilderness

CHRIS JOHNS, NATIONAL GEOGRAPHIC PHOTOGRAPHER

Handicapped Outdoor Group, an Idaho outfit founded by a man who lost his foot in an automobile accident.

These and other organizations are getting thousands of those with special needs to take part in even such unlikely activities as downhill skiing. "How do I describe the adrenaline-filled moments when I sensed that I was about to exceed, and finally expand, personal preset limits?" a quadriplegic wrote of his first downhill skiing effort. "How do I describe the peace that filled me in the monarchic splendor of the mountain, especially when I have been reminded too often that mountains were now unreachable?"

Once, at the very beginning of human history, we understood that the natural world was our home. It fed and clothed us and gave us our spiritual cosmos, a sense of connection to the life all around us, harmony. Even if we changed it with our agriculture and our earthen cities, so long as we respected the limits that the natural world imposed, so long as we did our best to maintain the

PAUL CHESLEY

harmony that sustained and enriched it, we were, as the Navajo say, "walking in beauty."

"The universal instructions of the Creator are universal and valid for all time," a Hopi elder once wrote. "The essence of these instructions is compassion for all life and love for all creation. We must realize that we do not live in a world of dead matter, but a universe of living spirit." Indeed, for many Native Americans, the earth itself, the very soil, had power.

"The Lakota was a true naturist—a lover of nature," wrote Chief Luther Standing Bear, who taught at the Rosebud Reservation in South Dakota in the 1880s. "He loved the earth and all things of the earth, the attachment growing with age. The old people came literally to love the soil and they sat or reclined on the ground with a feeling of being close to a mothering power. It was good for the skin to touch the earth and the old people liked to remove their moccasins and walk with bare feet on the sacred earth. Their tipis were built upon the earth and their altars were made of earth. The birds that flew in the air came to rest upon the earth and it was the final abiding place of all things that lived and grew. The soil was soothing, strengthening, cleansing and healing."

WHETHER WE ARE STILL ABLE to find that level of harmony with the world is something that may be open to question, given all the encumbrances—also called conveniences—with which we have saddled ourselves of late. It may be a perfection we will never reach, but perhaps the journey is as important as the goal itself. Aldo Leopold, the person who defined the respect we should pay to the natural world and its creatures, believed this perfection to be unattainable. "We shall never achieve harmony with land," he wrote in his journals once, "any more than we shall achieve justice or liberty for people. In these higher aspirations the important thing is not to achieve, but to strive."

In striving, then, we can still walk in beauty, and if so, the national lands give us our most enduring pathways. "In these areas it is as though a person were looking backward into the ages and forward untold years," wrote Harvey Broome, a colleague of Aldo Leopold and one of the founders of the Wilderness Society. "Here are bits of eternity, which have a preciousness beyond all accounting.…May they remain for all time—islands in time and in space, where living men can detach themselves from their civilization, and walk into eternity."

DURING A QUIET MOMENT *at Two Ocean Falls on the Continental Divide Trail in Wyoming's Bridger-Teton National Forest, horse-packing campers get a fire going while their mounts graze on trailside greenery (opposite).*

FOLLOWING PAGES: *Standing at the base of a steamy geothermal cascade, a fisherwoman casts her line in the Firehole River at Yellowstone National Park. Although fishing, camping, and other recreation on the national lands has a value that can be measured in hundreds of billions of dollars in fees and other revenues, the serenity of such interludes as those shown here are measurable only in the currency of the spirit.*
PAUL CHESLEY

BREATH STEAMING *in the morning chill, bull elk breakfast in a mountain meadow of* Yellowstone *National Park. One of the particularly compelling attractions of Yellowstone—perhaps*

SHIN YOSHINO/MINDEN PICTURES

more so here than in any other unit of the national lands system—is the opportunity it provides to observe at relatively close hand such large animals as elk, bighorn sheep, grizzly bears, and bison.

Looking to the Future

From Alaska TO FLORIDA,

FROM HAWAII TO MAINE, PRESERVING

NATURAL AMERICA MEANS MAKING HARD CHOICES

BETWEEN WHAT HUMAN BEINGS DESIRE AND

WHAT THE LAND CAN GIVE—CHOICES THAT AWAIT US

AS WE LOOK TO THE FUTURE.

. . . .

THEIR FUTURE AT STAKE: *El Capitan looms above its reflection in the Merced River in California's Yosemite National Park (opposite). A little grass frog (above) clings to a slender perch in a freshwater bog on Georgia's Cumberland Island National Seashore.* 125

MARC MUENCH (OPPOSITE); RAYMOND GEHMAN (ABOVE)

SPIKY TUFA FORMATIONS
poke above the surface of California's
Mono Lake, a salty body in Inyo National
Forest in the eastern Sierra. Since 1940,
water diversion has lowered the lake
nearly 44 feet. Environmentalists won
changes in water policy in 1989.

LARRY CARVER

BOZEMAN is a small university town in the Gallatin River valley of southwestern Montana. It is a nice town on its own merits, but what makes it especially attractive to me is the fact that on every horizon rise the humps and peaks that constitute much of the front range of the Rockies. The Bridgers, the Gallatin Range, the Madison Range, the Bitterroots, the Absarokas—all the lovely, round-shouldered peaks I see from my windows at home or while driving to classes at Montana State University—are embraced by the National Forest System as units of Gallatin and Beaverhead National Forests. They are just part of the sweep of national lands surrounding Bozeman, and more national forests, most with designated wilderness areas tucked into them, are within easy driving distance.

Other types of national lands are also relatively near to hand. Five hours or so to the northeast, the Missouri River curves magnificently through a few hundred thousand acres of Bureau of Land Management land. As it backs up behind Fort Peck Dam, the river is flanked on both sides by the 897,129 acres of the Charles M. Russell National Wildlife Range, a unit of the National Wildlife Refuge System. Down near the northeastern border of Idaho lies Red Rock Lakes National Wildlife Refuge, where some 300 trumpeter swans live year-round and are joined by many more in the winter, and south of the refuge lies the BLM's Centennial Mountains Wilderness Study Area. Finally, just a little under two hours away to the south of Bozeman is the ancestral national park—Yellowstone.

Attractive as all these landscapes are, what is of concern here are the types of activities taking place on, in, and around them, activities and land-use practices that can have either beneficial or detrimental effects on the long-term viability of these national preserves. The difficulty arises in assessing whether a given practice is ultimately good or bad for the land—or good or bad for the human communities tied to the land. As with most issues involving human beings, that assessment depends on where you live, how you earn your livelihood, what you value, and to whom you talk.

Nearly every morning, the front page of the *Bozeman Daily Chronicle* is noteworthy less for what it tells us of national politics or celebrity scandals than for what it has to say about public land-use issues, stories that not only get equal coverage but also often dominate the local news. In recent issues, for instance, the front page of the *Chronicle* has revealed that the Crown Butte Mining Company appears to have agreed to a deal with the owner of some private land that will enable the federal government to buy out the company's interest in a proposed gold mine on the northern edge of Yellowstone National Park, thus eliminating the risk of pollution in the park. The paper also reported that the National Park Service has acceded to petition from environmental activists to conduct a study on snowmobile use in Yellowstone to determine the impact of the machines on resident wildlife; the paper also noted that snowmobilers are worried that the study will reduce their access to the park. And in Wyoming, the paper said, state game officials are entertaining the idea of instituting a limited bison hunt on Bridger-Teton National Forest and National Elk Refuge land in order to reduce the size of the herd and its impact on the region's grasslands.

These are not headlines one would expect to see in the *New York Times* or the *St. Louis Post-Dispatch*, except on occasion. In Montana, they are common. Here, as in many other states where national lands and human ambitions collide, decisions are being made whose impacts will be felt for generations. These are the arenas in which we, the people, and our institutions are working, however imperfectly, to achieve a truly sustainable dynamic between what is demanded of the land and what it can give, and what human beings strive for and what we cannot have without putting the whole in peril. And as we all are learning, the task is as complex and difficult as it is necessary.

June 1, 1997: It was 4:30 in the morning when my wife and I joined the rest of the expedition in front of the Post Office in Mammoth, the National Park Service-controlled community in Yellowstone National Park. We had gotten up at 3 a.m. in Bozeman in order to be there on time, and we were both bleary-eyed from lack of sleep. No matter: We were here to see gray wolves—*Canis lupus*—and there was little we would not have endured for that extraordinary privilege.

What we endured, together with the ten or fifteen other eager folk herded along by a young wolf biologist, was a long, dark drive through the park, followed by an even longer hike from our parked vans and a steep climb up to the top of a knob overlooking a wide bench. By the time we reached the top of the knob, a gray blush of morning light had spread across the land. Pointing to a tiny, dark smear down on the bench, the biologist told us it was the carcass of an elk. The local den of wolves had killed it just the day before and sooner or later the animals would be by for a snack. It was windy and cold, the sky heavy with clouds, as we settled down to wait.

*carved into the stone of
South Dakota's Mount
Rushmore National
Memorial (opposite)
represents a president
who had a role in the
history of the American
national lands. George
Washington helped
forge the nation that
laid claim to them,
and Thomas Jefferson
enlarged this bounty
with the Louisiana
Purchase of 1803.
Abraham Lincoln
then signed legislation
giving millions of acres
of the purchase away
to railroads, states,
and homesteaders. In
the early years of the
century, however,
Theodore Roosevelt
saved millions of
acres for posterity by
establishing some of
the national forests,
national wildlife
refuges, and national
monuments still in
existence today.*

And wait. Well over an hour passed before someone spoke up in a loud whisper: "There—over to the left!" Led by a big animal so dark as to appear nearly black, four wolves emerged from a grove of ponderosa pine and trotted single file along the plateau, heading toward the carcass with dignified speed. Once there, they fed, each taking his or her turn as wolf protocol dictated. A couple of the young wolves engaged in mock combat, another appeared to nap. Even seen through powerful spotting scopes, the wolves were hardly larger than animated dots, but the thrill of contact was no less profound. We were looking at animals that had not been seen in this park for many decades. By the mid-1920s, a deliberate government program had wiped them out on the grounds that wolves were "bad" predators that not only slaughtered elk but also were perceived to be a major threat to the livestock industry. Almost 70 years later, a deliberate government program had brought them back. Everyone on that hilltop was smiling from ear to ear, for the creatures we were looking at represented nothing short of a bureaucratic miracle.

THE MIRACLE HAD begun with passage of the Endangered Species Act in 1973. The act stipulated that plant and animal populations found to be in danger of imminent extinction were to be restored to a healthy condition in their natural habitat— "recovered," as the act describes the process—and it was not much of a step beyond that to include the process of "reintroduction" in the equation. By the early 1980s the idea of reintroducing wolves to Yellowstone was gaining strength: The government had developed a recovery plan, and conservation organizations including the Defenders of Wildlife, the Greater Yellowstone Coalition, and the Wilderness Society were lining up behind the idea.

The livestock industry, however, was no more fond of gray wolves in the 1980s and 1990s than it had been in the 1880s and 1890s. Industry organizations and political supporters also lined up—in vigorous opposition to the idea of reintroducing a creature they claimed could eat the industry out of business. In the end, a controversial compromise was reached to allow the shooting of renegade wolves, and a compensation fund was established by the Defenders of Wildlife to pay ranchers for any cattle or sheep that could be proved to have been killed by wolves. In January 1995, three families of gray wolves were trapped in Canada and brought to Yellowstone, where they were put in scattered holding pens for a while. On January 12 they were released, pack by pack, into the wild, where they now number about 85 animals, only a few short of the hundred or so that were set as the goal to ensure a stable population. The healthy number has held in spite of a few deaths resulting from territorial fights, together with two sanctioned

PAUL CHESLEY

shootings of renegade wolves and five unsanctioned shootings of other wolves by renegade humans. By late 1997, the Defenders of Wildlife Compensation Fund had paid the livestock industry $7,700 for 4 calves, 12 ewes, and 53 lambs, out of a total livestock population in the region of more than 400,000 cattle and sheep.

Despite its success, the Yellowstone wolf recovery program has remained a matter of high controversy. In December 1997, a federal judge in Wyoming deemed the reintroduction program unlawful and ordered the wolves removed. The Interior Department was allowed to delay removal of the animals pending an expected appeal of the ruling by environmentalists.

Meanwhile, a similar effort has brought red wolves back to

Alligator River National Wildlife Refuge in North Carolina, and to Great Smoky Mountains National Park on the Tennessee-North Carolina border. Like the wolf reintroduction program in Yellowstone, this effort also engendered public controversy before being allowed to get under way.

CHRIS JOHNS, NATIONAL GEOGRAPHIC PHOTOGRAPHER (BOTH)

Resolving the needs of the land and the needs (or at least the desires) of human beings has always been a nettlesome matter, a confused mix of passion, advocacy, ignorance, traditional economics, and public impulses. At the national level, presidential administrations and Congresses come and go, each bringing with it a fresh set of national land priorities. These in turn prod federal agencies first in one direction, then in another, leaving the agencies often squabbling among and within themselves over land-management policies and responsibilities.

Adding to the confusion are the demands of a public with a wide range of views on the issues. On the one hand are various industries, special-interest groups, and private-property and free-enterprise organizations, each seeking exemptions to or massive changes in more restrictive environmental laws, such as the Clean Air and Clean Water Acts and the Endangered Species Act, or lobbying to retain such laws as the General Mining Law of 1872, which has no environmental restrictions. Groups and organizations on this side of the debate want permission to do a number of things on a long wish list: Increase logging; build roads into roadless areas; expand livestock grazing; allow oil rigs, gold mines, and coal mines to be developed in potential wilderness areas; increase the opportunity for off-road vehicle use and snowmobile travel; let private fossil hunters harvest paleontological resources on public lands.

O N THE OTHER HAND are conservation and environmental organizations of all sizes and stripes, sending their own teams to lobby Congress and the agencies for items on their own wish list: Wilderness designations, endangered-species protection, river protection, reductions in timber-cutting, prohibitions or rigid control of off-road vehicle use. These organizations testify before Congressional and agency committees. They publish reports, books, magazines, and newsletters, and produce videos and CD-ROMs. They establish Internet websites, and launch injunctions, lawsuits, appeals, and public protests. Sometimes they chain themselves to bulldozers.

In the West, where most of the national lands are, an added ingredient to the debate is the local resentment of "outsiders" who propose to tell longtime residents what they can and cannot do with what residents regard as their land. Particular anger is directed against federal land-managers so bold as to impose federal restrictions on federal land. This resentment surfaced during one of the public hearings in connection with Yellowstone wolf reintroduction. "This is a battlefield in a new civil war," said the executive director of the Cody, Wyoming, Chamber of Commerce, "the bicoastal areas against (Continued on page 142)

THE PATRON SAINT *of Florida's Everglades National Park was Marjory Stoneman Douglas (opposite), who published The Everglades: River of Grass in 1947 and spent most of the rest of her long life attempting to rescue the park from the kind of assaults illustrated by a warning sign in Florida Bay (below). In 1994, the federal government, the state, and the sugar industry forged an agreement that may bring the Everglades closer to salvation.*

EMERGING FROM AN EGG gently cracked by its mother, a newly hatched infant alligator climbs out of the maternal mouth to face the world in Everglades National Park. Once a badly threatened species, American alligators are on the rise again in protected coastal wetlands and estuaries.

CHRIS JOHNS, NATIONAL GEOGRAPHIC PHOTOGRAPHER

GLIDING THROUGH *a saw-grass swamp in Everglades National Park, a pair of explorers travel in craft built according to a Seminole Indian design. Most of the thousands of Seminole who once lived in*

CHRIS JOHNS, NATIONAL GEOGRAPHIC PHOTOGRAPHER

the region are gone now, and so are most of the millions of wading birds that once nested and bred in the Everglades, their habitat disturbed by changes in drainage and water-flow patterns.

NECKS STRAIGHT AS ARROWS,
*tundra swans fly in ragged formation over
North Carolina's Mattamuskeet National
Wildlife Refuge, where some 25,000 swans
winter every year. In the summer they head
north, many to Alaska's Arctic National
Wildlife Refuge, almost half a hemisphere
away. Both sanctuaries are crucial to
the survival of the species.*

JIM BRANDENBURG/MINDEN PICTURES

MIGRATING CARIBOU CROSS *the Kongakut River in Alaska's Arctic National Wildlife Refuge. The fate of the caribou is part of a national lands conservation battle. Preservationists want the*

GARY BRAASCH

adjacent coastal plain added to the refuge to preserve the caribou calving grounds and food sources. But the oil industry thinks as many as nine billion barrels of oil may lie underground there.

the West. Our battles are not Antietam or Gettysburg but the wolf, grazing, timber. This is a war on our culture, our way of life. And in this war the wolf is the nuclear weapon!"

Over the past several years, such contention has raised some land-use conflicts to the level of national debate, on a par with welfare reform and federal income-tax cuts. For example, the fate of the few remaining groves of old-growth forests in the national forests of the Pacific Northwest was the subject of nightly network television news, as one spokesperson after another expounded on the evils of environmentalism or the arrogance of the timber industry, while crowds waved placards in the background and anger seemed always ready to flame into physical violence. That issue was no sooner resolved— at least temporarily—by a compromise forest management plan than another eruption hit the air waves. This time the question was the advisability of "salvage sales" of downed or diseased timber in many of those same forests. Not long after that came the nationally-covered dispute over the slaughter of more than a thousand Yellowstone bison that had wandered out of the park in the winter of 1996-1997. The cattle industry feared the bison would spread brucellosis, a bovine disease that induces spontaneous abortion in cattle, although so far there has never been a documented case of bison transmitting brucellosis to cattle in a natural setting.

JIM BRANDENBURG

AS ALERT

as army sentinels, a trio of young great blue herons stand watch in New Mexico's Gila National Forest. They probably have less to fear than the tiny flock of nearly obliterated and still endangered whooping cranes clamming in Aransas National Wildlife Refuge, Texas (opposite).

Controversy piles upon controversy. In Utah's new 1.7-million-acre Grand Staircase-Escalante National Monument— whose very establishment in 1996 stirred resentment in much of the state—the Bureau of Land Management has approved a request from the Conoco Oil Company to begin drilling an exploratory oil well on a lease the company had acquired before the monument was established. Boosters of the local economy have cheered the BLM's consent; conservationists protest that it subverts the entire idea of the monument and that the government is simply gambling that the company will not find any oil— putting the land at stake in what it hopes is a long shot.

Nearly 3,000 miles north of Grand Staircase-Escalante, the 1.5 million acres of the coastal plain of Alaska's Arctic National Wildlife Refuge also are under threat of oil exploration. However, the government has so far resisted opening the area up to oil companies, who hope to find as much petroleum there as they did at Prudhoe Bay to the west nearly 30 years ago. Conservationists argue that the existence of commercial quantities of oil is questionable at best, and, whether oil is there or not, they want the coastal plain designated a wilderness area in order to

JAMES P. BLAIR

preserve its beauty and protect the tens of thousands of migrating caribou and other wild species that use it.

In Minnesota's 808,874-acre Boundary Waters Canoe Area Wilderness, meanwhile, the issue in contention is not oil, but access—motorized access. As stipulated by the Wilderness Act, most of the lakes in this watery wilderness are open to "paddle only" boats; here, canoeing is the principal means of transportation. Now, however, some local people and their congressional representatives say that current and proposed restrictions on motorized boats discriminate against women, children, older people, and those with physical disabilities that make it hard for them to get around in canoes. Conservationists argue that most people in fact can use canoes, whether female, young, old, or even, to a remarkable extent, disabled, a claim backed up by Wilderness Inquiry, an outfit that takes people of all kinds into the Boundary Waters and elsewhere. The fight to allow increased motorized access in one of the country's oldest designated wilderness areas continues.

VIRTUALLY EVERY STATE in the Union that possesses one or more units of national lands regularly experiences the eruption of such conflicts. Should we allow titanium mining in and around Okefenokee National Wildlife Refuge in Georgia and Florida? Should there be river mining in Alaska? Should we allow more beach recreation in piping plover nesting areas of Parker River National Wildlife Refuge on Plum Island in Massachusetts? Expand the timber cut in Colorado's national forests? Ban grazing in fragile riverine areas of BLM lands? Allow more resort development near the South Rim of Grand Canyon National Park to relieve tourist pressure on the South Rim itself? Approve a huge waste landfill next door to Joshua Tree National Park? Buy another 7,400 acres of California forest to preserve old-growth redwoods? Formulating the answers to these and a multitude of similar questions is a full-time job, and it seems likely the management of the national lands will continue to be punctuated by such item-by-item conflicts for years to come.

Happily, the convoluted process does not always result in bad news for the national lands. In August 1993, for example, Congress passed the Colorado Wilderness Act, placing 611,730 acres of national forest land in the National Wilderness Preservation System. In May 1994, Florida Governor Lawton Chiles signed into law the Everglades Forever Act, legislation that finally resolved a longstanding crusade by environmentalists and the federal government to force Florida's sugar industry to begin cleaning up the pollution it has caused in the watershed of Everglades National Park. In October of that same year, Congress passed the California Desert Protection Act, which not only designated another 7.5 million acres of wilderness but also upgraded Joshua Tree and Death Valley national monuments to national park status and established the Mojave National Preserve. And as recently as the fall of 1996, Congress passed an Omnibus Parks Act that included provisions to establish the Opal Creek Wilderness Area in Oregon's much-abused Willamette National Forest and the Tallgrass Prairie National Preserve in Kansas; the act also allocated funds for the purchase of the Sterling Forest in New York State.

The managers of many of the national parks have been taking a long, hard look at management practices and coming up with plans designed to return as much of their parkland as possible to a condition that approaches the natural state. At Grand Canyon, for instance, private automobiles will be banned from most of the park's roads, especially at the much visited and overstressed South Rim, and a light-rail system is being contemplated to reduce the impact of motor vehicles to near zero. The plan for Yosemite envisions that day-visitors would leave their cars in nearby towns and board regional buses that would drop them off at a park shuttle station for transport inside the park. In addition, after a terrible flood washed away several original campgrounds and lodge units along the Merced River in January 1997, national park officials decided not to rebuild them. A busing system is also planned for Utah's Zion National Park, as well as for Maine's Acadia. Elsewhere, park managers have decided to eliminate certain amenities, restoring the land to a more natural state. In California, for instance, 180 miles of logging roads are being removed from Redwood National Park, and in Minnesota some 400 cabins and other structures are going to be torn down in Voyageurs National Park. In all, nearly one-third of the nation's parks are going to be "remodeled" along more natural lines. The decision echoes the dictum of former National Park Service Director William Penn Mott that if we are going to err with regard to the national parks, "we must err on the side of preservation."

One way or the other, much is being done to resolve some of the more complex issues that afflict the national lands system, and there is even the possibility that future management policies will help to bring down the incidence of conflict. A growing number of people think it is time to address conservation issues on a broader and more comprehensive scale, to forestall disputes in the future over what constitutes use and misuse. Such an effort would attempt to weld science, economic and land-use planning, local community concerns, and environmentalism from the grassroots to the national level with the oversight functions of local, state, and federal government agencies. The anticipated result would be an administrative matrix that might assure a stable future for the national lands and the communities of life contained within them, including human communities. The notion is an ambitious one, certainly, replete with its own set of problems. But, however haltingly and imperfectly, it is being acted out at one level or another in many areas of the country where land and people meet most dramatically.

In the Greater Yellowstone Ecosystem, for example, about 14 million acres of national lands in Montana, Idaho, and Wyoming embrace a total of two national parks, three national wildlife refuges, part or all of seven national forests, as well as some forty designated wilderness areas, wilderness study areas, and proposed wilderness areas. The region includes several major river systems and too many lakes to count, with many species of trout and other fishes. Forests of lodgepole pine, Douglas fir, aspen, spruce, and many other tree species abound. There are scores of bird species and populations of grizzlies, black bears, mountain lions, bison, wolves, mule deer, elk, coyotes, and other large mammals, none of which pays the least attention to the designation of the land it wanders through, whether park, forest, or refuge.

PETER ESSICK

The belief that such distinctions are irrelevant, that the individual parts cannot intelligently be separated out from the whole, inspired the formation of the Greater Yellowstone Coalition (GYC) at the Teton Science School in Moose, Wyoming, in 1983. The GYC—a collection of local environmentalists and such national conservation organizations as the Wilderness Society, the National Audubon Society, and the National Wildlife Federation—was instrumental in persuading Congress to hold hearings in 1985 to investigate management practices in the Greater Yellowstone region. In the end, conservationists did not achieve their goal of establishing an overall management authority for the ecosystem. However, the hearings did prompt the Greater Yellowstone Coordinating Committee— a body that includes the superintendents of Yellowstone and Grand Teton National Parks and the heads of the three national wildlife refuges and the seven national forests of the region—to collect research from the various agencies for inclusion in a single database. "For the first time," the manager of Red Rock Lakes National Wildlife Refuge told a reporter in 1987, "you have a chance to look at timber cuts of the Targhee, for example, as compared to the Shoshone or the Beaverhead. Or how many moose Bridger-Teton has compared to Red Rock. It may be a crude resource, but it's the first opportunity we've had to see what is where in this ecosystem."

Crude or not, the coordinating committee of the Greater Yellowstone Ecosystem (GYE) was the first serious effort to get federal agencies to begin thinking about how they might join together to manage an entire land system. According to Yellowstone Park historian Paul Schullery, that in itself was a major step forward. Now, as he writes in *Searching for Yellowstone*, "the National Park Service is routinely involved in regional planning. The park's connections to the rest of the GYE, made clear by the wanderings of grizzly bears, the migrations of elk and bison, and geothermal aquifers that cross park boundaries in many directions, are now seen as giving Yellowstone superintendents a strong mandate to speak out on issues affecting the GYE."

THE MANAGEMENT practices evolving for the Greater Yellowstone Ecosystem are still vulnerable to conflicting visions about what should or should not be allowed in the way of recreation, logging, road-building, mining, and other uses. Conflicts in 1997 alone included an uproar over the killing of bison, controversy over potential pollution from the Crown Butte Mine, and concern over Park Service attempts to study the effects of snowmobile use on wildlife populations. Even with the ecosystem concept firmly in place, finding the middle ground of management that will satisfy everyone remains dauntingly difficult.

Nevertheless, it seems clear that such large visions of management may be the wave of the conservation future. They are what drove the government to direct the U.S. Forest Service and the Bureau of Land Management in 1993 to come up with a management plan for more than 22 million acres of federal forestland in the Pacific Northwest that would be "scientifically sound, ecologically credible, and legally responsible." Most conservation groups complained that the resulting plan still put too much old-growth forest at risk from logging and road-building. Without the plan, however, traditional management could have obliterated within a few years the last remaining groves of old-growth forests and the populations of northern spotted owls, marbled murrelets, and other species dependent on them. *(Continued on page 154)*

THE SPINNING TEETH *of a logger's chain saw bite through a choice Port Orford cedar in Oregon's Siskiyou National Forest (opposite).*

FOLLOWING PAGES: *In Washington's Okanogan National Forest, a worker using a drip torch sets a pile of slash on fire to prepare a clear-cut for replanting. For more than a century, the old-growth forests of the Pacific Northwest have been a mainstay of the timber industry. Now only a small remnant of the original national forest old-growth remains, and the fight to preserve it has involved the federal government in an agonizing mix of social, ecological, and economic problems.*

PETER ESSICK

(Continued on page 154)

SUNRISE MIST DRIFTS

over trees in Boundary Waters Canoe Area Wilderness in Minnesota's Superior National Forest. Although one national lands unit lies within the other, the wilderness area has a fire management policy based on allowing natural fires to maintain the system's health. The general policy in Superior National Forest, on the other hand, is to put fires out.

RAYMOND GEHMAN

BAWLING AND KICKING UP DUST, *a herd of cattle moves along Bureau of Land Management grazing land near Orovada, Nevada. Almost as much metaphorical dust has been raised*

PAUL CHESLEY

by controversy over the use of public grazing lands, but in at least a few areas, environmentalists and the cattle industry are attempting to resolve the issues that divide them.

INTRICATE
GEOMETRY
of the Pueblo Bonito
ruin in New Mexico's
Chaco Culture
National Historical
Park suggests that its
builders developed a
relatively complex
society. Chaco Canyon
is threatened on two

A similar largeness of vision inspired the Department of the Interior to work with the state of California, the San Diego Association of Governments, and private landowners to come up with a development plan built upon ecosystem principles. Ideally, the "Natural Communities Conservation Plan" would allow for continued urban and suburban development in one of the fastest-growing regions of the country, and at the same time preserve a significant portion of remaining coastal sage scrub habitat— some of it federally owned, some state owned, some city owned, and a great deal privately owned—as habitat for the threatened California gnatcatcher and several other species. Many conservationists worried that too much control at the local level ultimately

ROBERT E. BARBER

would undermine the effectiveness of the preservation effort, and some scientists expressed uncertainty whether anything would be enough to save the gnatcatcher. But Secretary of the Interior Bruce Babbitt expressed the hope in 1993 that the plan might "become an example of what must be done across the country if we are to avoid the environmental and economic train wrecks we've seen in the last decade."

Rather more uncertainty applies to another experiment in the Golden State, an experiment in what might be called "bioregional conservation." The land at issue here is the entire Sierra Nevada, about 400 miles of mountain-range ecology that includes eight national forests, three national parks, some twenty wilderness areas,

sides by proposed strip mining for coal, and the ruins could face potential damage from erosion. According to environmental activists, unprotected ruins outside the park also are at risk of being heavily damaged or completely destroyed.

BRIGHT
CLUTCH

*of eggs nestles on
Pelican Island National
Wildlife Refuge,
Florida (opposite). This
sandy two-acre dot off
the state's east coast
was set aside as a bird
sanctuary for brown
pelicans and other
species in 1903 by
the executive order of
President Theodore
Roosevelt, who thus
began the National
Wildlife Refuge System.
Eastern populations of
brown pelicans, once
faced with extinction
because of DDT build-
up in their eggs, are
now classed as "fully
recovered," thanks to a
federal ban on the use
of DDT, and a recovery
program mandated by
the Endangered Species
Act of 1973.*

seven wild and scenic rivers, the Pacific Crest Trail, and a good deal of scattered BLM land. The Sierra Nevada also has been logged, mined, grazed, and otherwise utilized diligently for almost a century and a half. Today, real estate development and road-building has brought an urban character to its foothill country that contributes traffic congestion, strip malls, and even air pollution. Huge, sprawling, complicated by a plethora of counties and cities whose economic foundations range from tourism to second-home development, and from skiing to mining, the Sierra Nevada seems an unlikely candidate for unified management theories. Nonetheless, an attempt is being made. This time the impetus comes from an agglomeration of entities, some of whom in the past would have found themselves adversaries rather than allies: the Sierra Business Council, the Sierra Nevada Alliance, the Sierra Now Conference, and the Wilderness Society and other conservation groups. Tacit, if somewhat nervous, support comes from state and federal land-management agencies.

IN 1993, Congress stepped into the picture by appropriating seven million dollars to finance a study of the economic, political, social, and ecological issues challenging the Sierra. Called the Sierra Nevada Ecosystem Project (SNEP), the study team issued its 3,000-page report in June 1996. The report proposed no solutions, or even any firm guidelines about what ought to be done and how to do it. However, the study did make clear the dimensions of the problems afflicting the Sierra and the incontrovertible need to address its future as a single entity and in a unified way, unfragmented by contradictory impulses.

Ultimately, such large-scale management notions may or may not succeed in shaping a new future for the national lands of the Sierra Nevada, and the Pacific Northwest, and coastal southern California, and the Greater Yellowstone, and anywhere else that similar efforts are either under way or being discussed. But even the possibility of preserving the national heritage of land brings with it a species of hope. Richard Reinhardt, a reporter covering the Sierra effort, saw a man break down in tears at one point when faced with the enormity of the effort involved in saving the forests of the mountains. When Reinhardt saw the man again at the press conference announcing the release of the SNEP report, "he was smiling and taking notes vigorously on a clipboard." As Reinhardt put it, "His spirits, like mine, had rebounded to the light. He was seeing again the Big Picture, the future beyond the fallen trees."

FARRELL GREHAN

WILD PONIES *feed on protein-rich marsh and dune grasses on the narrow barrier island of Chincoteague National Wildlife Refuge off the eastern shore of Virginia. The shy creatures are a*

RAYMOND GEHMAN

powerful draw, helping attract more than a million visitors a year and making Chincoteague one of the nation's most heavily visited wildlife refuges, a popularity that endangers the island's fragile ecosystems.

The Library of Life

OUR NATIONAL LANDS

ARE RICH IN A PRICELESS ARRAY

OF PLANTS AND ANIMALS

—A VERITABLE LIBRARY OF LIFE—

FROM WHICH WE HAVE MUCH

STILL TO LEARN.

• • • • • • • • • • • • • • • • • •

FLOURISHING DIVERSITY: *In the treetops of Oregon's Willamette National Forest, a researcher examines lichens as part of a canopy study (opposite). A spear of endangered Haleakala silversword blooms in Haleakala National Park, Hawaii (above).* 161

GARY BRAASCH (OPPOSITE); CHRIS JOHNS, NATIONAL GEOGRAPHIC PHOTOGRAPHER (ABOVE)

COLORFUL HIGH COUNTRY
*wildflowers bloom in a meadow backed
by the striking profile of Scapegoat
Mountain in Montana's Lewis and Clark
National Forest. The bouquet of species
seen here includes lupines, paintbrushes,
and blanket flowers.*

DAVID MUENCH

WHEN I WAS A BOY, one of my favorite stories was about a group of 20th century Americans who travel back in time to the age of the dinosaurs. While there, one of the time travelers ignores the regulations imposed by the "tour company," steps off the path he is supposed to stay on, and accidentally kills a small, seemingly insignificant creature hardly bigger than a mouse. When the travelers are beamed back to modern times, they find that their entire society has changed: A dictator rules the land, freedom is gone, life is a misery. All, the story implies, because one tiny creature in the chain of evolution had been wiped out, thereby altering the future.

Although such direct—and dire—consequences of a single extinction may be unlikely, this cautionary tale is worth thinking about. Even as you read these words, one of the great mass extinctions of species in the world's history is proceeding apace. The destruction and fragmentation of habitat across the world by human actions has raised the rate of species extinction hundreds of times above levels that might be considered normal in evolutionary terms. Knowing just what might have been "normal" in the remote past is difficult; gaps in the fossil record mean we can't know what was lost. However, one cautious estimate puts the ancient background level of extinctions at a few species per type of organism (fish, for example, or mammals or birds), per million years. This routine average rate of loss ordinarily would be offset by the evolution of new species, resulting in no net loss in biological diversity.

Occasionally, though, this sustainable process has been punctuated by cataclysmic extinctions in which masses of species are wiped out in a relatively brief period of time. When this happens, David Quammen writes in *The Song of the Dodo: Island Biogeography in an Age of Extinctions*, "the extinction rate far exceeds the rate of speciation, and the richness of the biosphere plummets. Niches fall vacant. Intricate networks of ecological relationships are thrown into disarray. Entire ecosystems are left raw and ragged."

With pointed humor, Quammen puts the modern dilemma of the human impact on species in context. Eons in the future, he writes, paleontologists from another planet might look at earth and wonder what could have happened "to cause such vast losses so suddenly at six points in time: at the end of the Ordovician, in the late Devonian, at the end of the Permian, at the end of the

Triassic, at the end of the Cretaceous, and again about sixty-five million years later, in the late Quaternary, right around the time of the invention of the dugout canoe, the stone ax, the iron plow, the three-masted sailing ship, the automobile, the hamburger, the television, the bulldozer, the chain saw, and the antibiotic."

The processes of modern extinction are visible everywhere in the world, most notoriously in the species-rich rain forests of Brazil, where entomologist E. O. Wilson has estimated that the rate of extinction may be a thousand times greater than normal. In the United States we have been no less thoughtless. Since 1900, we have rendered extinct such creatures as the passenger pigeon, the dusky seaside sparrow, and the Carolina parakeet. We have also put more than 1,100 native plant and animal species at such risk that they are listed as either endangered or threatened. Under the stipulations of the Endangered Species Act of 1973, "endangered" species are faced with immediate extinction if nothing is done to help them; "threatened" species are at serious risk of being placed on the endangered list. The desert pupfish, Lange's metalmark butterfly, the small whorled pogonia, the Florida panther, the red-cockaded woodpecker, the Chisos Mountain hedgehog cactus— these and scores of other species scattered from the Hawaiian Islands to the Florida Keys, the Maine woods to the California desert, are facing evolutionary oblivion in the United States.

The loss of any species is regrettable for its own sake. The loss of an entire kind of life leaves an especially forlorn hole in the earth's mantle of existence. But species loss is important for another reason, too, as President Richard Nixon hinted when he signed the Endangered Species Act in 1973. "Nothing is more priceless," he said, "...than the rich array of animal life with which our country has been blessed. It is a many-faceted treasure, of value to scholars, scientists, and nature lovers alike, and it forms a vital part of the heritage we all share as Americans." In truth, the phrase should read "rich array of animal and plant life," but in either form it suggests something that has come to be called biodiversity. Defined as the variety of life and its processes, biodiversity includes all lifeforms, from the smallest virus to the giant sequoia, and the natural functions that link them, up and down the food chain.

Biodiversity has been described as occurring on four levels— genetic, species, community, and landscape diversity. The most familiar is species diversity, which refers to the number of species in a given area needed to produce a healthy, functioning ecosystem. Genetic diversity is the level below species diversity, and refers to preserving the variation within species—that is, distinct populations and genes. When we lose whole populations of trees,

TOM BEAN

for example through forest-management practices that weed out unwanted species or plant "improved" seedlings, we lose the basic variety that drives evolution. With the loss of genetic diversity, which occurs when populations of a given species dwindle and become isolated, species can no longer adapt to changing conditions. The two levels above species diversity are community, which refers to an assemblage of species in a given place, and landscape diversity, the geography of different ecosystems across a large area and the way they are connected. By conserving community diversity, we preserve unique interrelationships of species and ensure both conservation of species and preservation of some genetic diversity. The relationships among landscape elements— forest patches and watersheds, for example—and the communities within them determine what species will inhabit the particular landscape. For some species, the size of the patches of habitat and intact migration routes are also critical.

JUST HOW MANY species are necessary to maintain a healthy ecosystem tends to vary from system to system, and there is considerable debate among scientists today over whether the number of different species is as important as which species they are and the ways they interact with one another. According to British ecologist Dr. Phil Grime, "There are often just a few animals and a few plants that are really running the show, and what happens to them is really crucial." Dr. Peter Kareiva of the University of Washington counters that sheer variety is still important: "The studies show that species richness does matter. It's like an insurance policy. The more species you have, the more likely you are to have the right ones. The more you eliminate, the more likely you are to have eliminated some particular function."

Scientific opinion may be divided on the question of how many species are enough, but it is clearly united in its concern about species extinction and in its conviction that biodiversity, however one measures it, is something to be desired. Significant levels of biodiversity, in fact, are what helped another team of scientists, sponsored by the Canadian and United States branches of the World Wildlife Fund, determine which "ecoregions" in North America should be the focus of concern. The team announced in September 1997 that the North American continent included 32 ecoregions that contained "biodiversity that elevates them to a globally outstanding ranking." This finding came as something of a surprise. "We always tend to (Continued on page 172)

FLOWERING BROMELIADS *bring a touch of flame to the tropical, woody green tangle of Puerto Rico's Caribbean National Forest (opposite), home to 240 native tree species and more than 50 bird species, including the endangered Puerto Rican parrot.*

FOLLOWING PAGES: *On a mossy branch in Oregon's temperate Willamette National Forest, a spotted owl clutches a mouse in its talon. An ornithologist has used the mouse as bait so that he can study the owl—one of the major "indicator species" by which scientists measure the health of the old-growth ecosystem.*

GARY BRAASCH

"JUMPING" CHOLLAS *spread in profusion over the landscape in the Cactus Garden of California's Joshua Tree National Park. Established as a national monument in 1936, Joshua Tree was*

CARR CLIFTON/MINDEN PICTURES

enlarged and upgraded to national park status in 1994, largely in recognition of its value as a repository of desert species such as the Joshua tree, smoke tree, cholla, desert ironwood, and ocotillo.

SCARLET 'I'IWI

*(opposite) illustrates
one of the principles of
species diversity in
isolation. One of the 50
species of Hawaiian
honeycreeper that
evolved from a single
finchlike ancestral
species to fill every
available ecological
niche, the 'i'iwi has a
slender, curved beak
adapted for sipping
nectar from long-
throated native lobelia.
The state's two national
parks and ten national
wildlife refuges offer
some protection to the
remaining 21 species
of honeycreeper—
two-thirds of which are
on the endangered list,
threatened by avian
malaria and the
destruction of
their habitat.*

equate biodiversity only with places like Brazil, or Indonesia," Dr. Eric Dinerstein, senior scientist at the World Wildlife Fund, told the *New York Times*. "But as you look more deeply, you begin to realize that it's as if North Americans have won the biological lottery, but forgot to look at the ticket." The many ecoregions under discussion in the World Wildlife Fund report include the Sierra Nevada forests of California, the mixed forests of the Appalachian Mountains from Georgia to Pennsylvania, and the southeastern mixed forests from Virginia to Alabama. All contain significant portions of the national lands system, which, despite the problems that beset them—from the clear-cutting of their timber to the pollution of their streams—remain the last best hope the United States has of preserving its own stake in the biodiversity lottery.

MANY PEOPLE ARE probably now aware that regions in the tropical zone of high humidity and constantly warm climate contain the richest collections of species. By one estimate, 2.5 acres of rain forest like that in Brazil might contain as many as 42,000 insect species. Scientist E. O. Wilson, whose specialty is ants, once discovered 43 distinct species of ants in a single tree in Peru. Less widely known, however, is that the national lands of the United States include tropical regions whose rich diversity of species is no less at risk than that of the Brazilian rain forest.

The Hawaiian Islands are a prime example. Of the more than 1,100 species on the endangered or threatened lists maintained by the U.S. Fish and Wildlife Service, more than 290 are located in Hawaii. Island ecosystems are peculiar: They are colonized by stray organisms, which then evolve in isolation; whatever organisms make their way to the island thus tend to radiate to fill all available ecological niches. In the Hawaiian Islands, one of the most isolated archipelagoes on earth, 96 percent of the native species are endemic, meaning they occur nowhere else on the planet. Before man came along, the only two mammals that had made their way across the ocean were the hoary bat and the monk seal. Insects and birds filled almost every niche. For example, some 50 species or subspecies of honeycreeper evolved in Hawaii from one ancestral finchlike species; more than half of those species are now extinct. The islands are also home to 364 species of Hawaiian fruit flies, with more awaiting identification.

Today, Hawaii's humid tree fern forests support some of the most diverse species of birds to be found anywhere in the world.

These include black-necked stilts, Hawaiian crows, and honey-creepers of a bewildering variety of shapes, sizes, colors, and songs. But these forests are being fragmented by agricultural and urban development and degraded by the onslaughts of feral pigs, which not only eat vegetation important to habitat but also eat and spread the seeds of invasive plants. Virtually the only true sanctuaries for Hawaii's birdlife, as well as for the Hawaiian monk seal and the Hawaiian hoary bat—both found nowhere else on earth and both listed as endangered—are provided by the state's relatively small national land units. These include two national parks—Haleakala on Maui and Hawaii Volcanoes on the Big Island of Hawaii—and ten national wildlife refuges, such as 917-acre Hanalei NWR on Kauai and 44-acre Kakahaia NWR on Molokai.

CHRIS JOHNS, NATIONAL GEOGRAPHIC PHOTOGRAPHER

Another American island—Puerto Rico—includes a rich repository of tropical species. The Caribbean National Forest, 28,000 acres of jungle surrounded by agricultural and urban development, is an island within the island. Despite its small size, Caribbean National Forest protects 32 reptile and amphibian species, such as the Puerto Rican boa constrictor, and about 240 native tree species. It is also a haven for more than 50 bird species, including species of bullfinches, tanagers, woodpeckers, and warblers found nowhere else on earth. The Puerto Rican parrot, once common all over the island, is listed as endangered, as are seven other bird species on the island.

On the mainland, tropical and temperate zones meet in southern Texas, where Laguna Atascosa National Wildlife Refuge hugs the coast of the Gulf of Mexico just north of the Rio Grande. From Brownsville to Rio Grande City, the Santa Ana National Wildlife

Refuge and the various units of the Lower Rio Grande Valley National Wildlife Refuge are also strung along the Rio Grande.

Biologists have referred to the entire area around the lower Rio Grande as a biological crossroads, bringing together species from the tropics, the temperate zone, the desert, and the Caribbean coastal wetlands. Here, olive sparrows, kiskadee flycatchers, white-tailed hawks, and another 30 species of tropical birds find the limits of their northern range, and both the lower river and the wetlands of Laguna Atascosa are winter home to hundreds of thousands of migrating birds from as far away as Alaska. In the river valley near Brownsville is a population of red-crowned parrots, avian immigrants from threatened habitat in Mexico; the last known breeding population of ocelots in the United States, numbering about a hundred, huddles in the chaparral of Laguna Atascosa and the lower Rio Grande Valley. In all, the lower Rio Grande area harbors 145 vertebrate species either threatened, endangered, or otherwise of "management concern" because of habitat loss. Since 1979, a coalition of the U.S. Fish and Wildlife Service, the state of Texas and various conservation groups has been trying to patch together a corridor of protected habitat sufficient to sustain viable populations of species. The goal is a 145-mile-long stretch along the Rio Grande that would extend from Falcon Dam in the west to the South Bay tidal flats near Brownsville before turning north toward Laguna Atascosa. So far, about half of the necessary acreage has been purchased.

ANOTHER ITEM on the American biodiversity lottery ticket is the Southern Appalachian Highlands, the stretch of the Appalachian Mountains that runs though portions of West Virginia, Virginia, North Carolina, Tennessee, South Carolina, and Georgia. Not so very long ago in the grand scheme of things, it was said that a squirrel could travel the canopy of the great eastern woodland from the Atlantic to the Mississippi without once touching the ground. Now, like most of the rest of the eastern forests, those of the Southern Appalachians have been logged over at least once, and sometimes twice. Rare pockets of old growth remain: a complex understory, with trees of all ages, including moss-covered, gnarled white oaks anywhere from 350 to 450 years old, whose branches, in the words of one poetic observer, "ripple sideways like braided hair undone."

Regrowth has been abundant, however. The 24 million acres of the Southern Appalachian Highlands—all within an easy drive of tens of millions of people—hold what forest ecologist R.H. Whittaker once called "one of the two great centers of forest diversity" in the United States. At its heart lie the 520,000 acres of Great Smoky Mountains National Park and 3.4 million acres of the region's 6 national forests, including Nantahala and Pisgah National Forests.

Spilling over the rolling old mountains in a rich, multilayered carpet, the forest mix contains more than 150 tree species. Among them are black oaks, red oaks, and white oaks; eastern white pines and flowering dogwoods; yellow poplars and eastern hemlocks; shagbark hickorys, maples, spruces, beeches, and birches. These and dozens more mix with an understory dominated by dark-leaved rhododendrons and mountain laurels, together with mosses, ferns, and 1,500 species of flowering plants. Animal life is no less diverse, including black bears, red foxes, and reintroduced red wolves who make a decent living from voles, chipmunks, and the occasional whitetail deer. Of 54 salamander species, 23 are endemic. In the canopy above, red-cockaded woodpeckers hammer tree trunks for insects, and red-eyed vireos and dark-eyed juncos go about their business on the forest floor. Southern flying squirrels sail from tree to tree, broad-winged hawks, red-tailed hawks, harriers, bald eagles, and golden eagles sail the skies, and several species of North American owls cruise the night.

This wonderfully varied natural landscape—as diverse as any in the United States—is also threatened. Logging continues in the national forests, fragmenting habitat and interrupting the natural succession of both plant and animal species. As a result, 12 vertebrate species are listed as endangered, including the Carolina northern flying squirrel, the red-cockaded woodpecker, and the Virginia big-eared bat. Six species are listed as threatened, including the spotfin chub and the slackwater darter, and 42 are recognized candidates for listing, including the northern pine snake and the southern water shrew.

Across the continent, the other "great center of forest diversity" rises just inland from the Pacific, a knot of upthrust rock in southwest Oregon and northwest California. The Siskiyou and the Klamath Mountains—which share the Siskiyou National Forest in southern Oregon and the Klamath National Forest in northern California—are home to species that live nowhere else, including Brewer spruce, Sadler's oak, and Port Orford cedar. The Klamath Mountains have more plant species than the Sierra or the Cascades, probably because they get more rain in the summer than the Sierra and have been less glaciated than either the Sierra or the Cascades. As a result, (Continued on page 187)

FOLLOWING PAGES: *A great egret, its wings nearly translucent in the sun, stalks through shallow water in Florida's J.N. "Ding" Darling National Wildlife Refuge on Sanibel Island. A Pulitzer Prize-winning editorial cartoonist and the refuge system's first great champion, Darling was named by Franklin D. Roosevelt to oversee the refuges in 1934. He not only enlarged the system by nearly 4 million acres in just 18 months, but also helped win passage of the Duck Stamp Act, which has since made millions of dollars available for the protection of wildfowl habitat.*

RAYMOND GEHMAN

GARY BRAASCH

JEFF FOOTT (BOTH)

GIVING SHELTER

to the more than 1,100 native plant and animal species that are in danger of extinction in America is one of the highest purposes of the national lands system. Such protection is by no means confined to the wildlife refuges; important sanctuaries are found in much of the rest of the national lands as well. The wood stork (opposite), for example, listed as endangered throughout its range from South Carolina to Alabama, has found a much needed

haven in Everglades National Park. The threatened desert tortoise (top), driven out of much of its range in southwestern Nevada and the northern California desert by cattle, off-road vehicles, and urban development, is dependent upon protected habitat set aside by the BLM in both states. Desert pupfish (above), at even greater risk than the tortoise, have been reduced by habitat loss to a few scattered populations, including some in Arizona's Organ Pipe Cactus National Monument.

SHAFTS OF SUNLIGHT *pierce the deep shade of a bald-cypress swamp in Illinois's Shawnee*
National Forest. Like other Midwestern states, Illinois has few national lands, but Shawnee, the lone

DAVID MUENCH

national forest, is home to more than 1,100 different kinds of flowering plants within its 273,000 acres.
Eight wildlife refuges round out the state's other national land units devoted to preserving natural values.

HEALTHY FRESHWATER MARSH,
*such as this one around the reedy shores of
Sullivan Bay in Minnesota's Voyageurs
National Park, utilizes, stores, and recycles
energy from the sun to create a highly
productive ecosystem. The Voyageurs
wetlands, for example, support diverse
animal life, including beavers, bald eagles,
and northern pike.*

DAVID MUENCH

CONTORTED BY TIME AND WIND, *a Great Basin bristlecone pine stands rooted to the arid slopes of the eastern Sierra Nevada in California's Inyo National Forest. These trees—some of them*

PAUL CHESLEY

more than 4,700 years old—are the embodiment of stubborn adaptability, sprouting and surviving for centuries in an environment that seems capable of supporting little more than lichens.

CARR CLIFTON/MINDEN PICTURES

conditions here may more closely resemble those of five to two million years ago, during the Pliocene Epoch.

This diversity has not gone unrecognized. In 1992, the Klamaths were identified by the International Union for the Conservation of Nature as one of seven areas in the United States—and one of 200 worldwide—to be of global botanical significance. Today, however, this significant locale is under constant pressure by the timber industry. The Port Orford cedar, for example, is vulnerable to a root-rot fungus that is spread by logging, roads, and livestock. Since 1980, the fungus has spread from Oregon into California's Smith River drainage, and the Port Orford cedar is on the verge of making the endangered list. The Oregon Siskiyous hold the last uninfected area of major size.

ALTHOUGH ONE EXPECTS biodiversity in the tropics, or even, to some degree, in the Pacific Northwest, the desert west seems a less accommodating cradle. However, the region of the California desert— spreading in a ragged rectangle behind greater metropolitan Los Angeles—includes a surprising range of habitats, from flat scrubland dotted with outcrops of lush riparian vegetation, to pockets of cool fir forests and, what is perhaps more expected, wind-sculpted sand dunes. With portions of the Mojave, Sonoran, and Great Basin desert systems overlapping one another, the region is home to two national parks, Joshua Tree and Death Valley, and one national preserve, Mojave. Strung along the Colorado River between California and Arizona are three national wildlife refuges—Cibola, Havasu, and Imperial—together with numerous designated BLM wilderness areas scattered from the Inyo Mountains of the north to the Jacumba Mountains on the border with Mexico.

The California desert is geologically young—which means that many of its rugged features have not yet been eroded or scoured down by wind and water. As a result, the terrain holds a wide variety of soil conditions and landforms, creating a remarkable diversity of climatic and ecological niches. Within these 25-million-or-so acres of mixed desert systems live an incredible number and variety of dryland and desert riparian species. And all are at risk, pinched by the relentless urban growth spreading north from Los Angeles and south from Las Vegas, growth that not only eats up unprotected land but adds recreational pressure on the fragile ecosystems protected as part of the national lands system. Here, amid the dunes and desert springs and boulder-piled,

BRIGHT PINK *rhododendron blossoms in northern California's Redwood National Park glow against the fog-shadowed trunks of soaring coast redwoods (opposite). The park holds only a remnant of the redwood groves that once ran along the Coast Ranges from Monterey north into Oregon. Nearly logged to extinction, the redwoods continue to be threatened. Many scientists fear that high levels of ozone, acid deposition, and other forms of pollution could ultimately bring the coast redwoods and many other tree species to ruin.*

ON THE BRINK
OF EXTINCTION,
*Utah prairie dogs
have been reduced by
shooting, poisoning, and
loss of habitat. Efforts
to restore a healthy
population of the species
are occurring in places
such as Bryce Canyon
National Park, where a
biologist traps a prairie
dog to mark it
(opposite). Once the
animal has been
released, scientists will
monitor its longevity,
reproduction, and
travel patterns. For
some species, such
restoration programs—
one imperative of the
Endangered Species
Act—are proving
successful: The U.S.
Fish and Wildlife
Service estimates that
about 41 percent of all
species currently listed
as endangered or
threatened are either
stable or improving.*

pastel-colored mountains, are some of the oldest living organisms known to earth: the gnarled bristlecone pines found in Inyo National Forest, alive for some 4,700 years, and the creosote bush clones that sit in huge circles in the Mojave Desert, some of them estimated to be anywhere from 10,000 to 12,000 years old. Here are Joshua trees and elephant trees; white bear poppies and black milk vetches; Barstow woolly-sunflowers, violet twining snapdragons and Kingston Mountain cinquefoils; spiny hedgehog cactuses; "jumping" chollas, and desert palms—more than 2,000 native plant species, about 200 of them found nowhere else in the world. The U.S. Fish and Wildlife Service lists 3 plants as endangered, 2 are considered threatened, and the service recognizes 10 species as likely candidates for the threatened list. The state of California—which, like many states, keeps its own listings—counts 7 species as endangered and considers 11 to be of "special concern."

The desert also provides refuge for nearly 650 vertebrate species, a zoological kaleidoscope that includes three species of desert bighorn sheep, San Joaquin kit foxes, kangaroo rats, desert tortoises, fringe-toed lizards, Gila monsters, slender salamanders, Inyo Mountain salamanders, whip-scorpions, Southwestern cave bats, big-eared bats, brown pelicans, golden eagles, burrowing owls, and willow flycatchers. Most of these are listed as endangered, threatened, or species of special concern by either the federal government or the state government. Meanwhile, six fish species, including the Owens pupfish and the Mojave tui chub, are listed as federally endangered. Clearly, for all its wide-open emptiness, heat, and aridity, the California desert is a remarkable garden of diversity; conserving this biological potpourri is crucial to preserving the natural integrity of one of the largest and most fragile natural systems in the United States.

Much has been left out of this "biological survey." The Florida Keys harbor small populations of tiny key deer, and South Florida has its endangered manatees. I haven't mentioned all the parks, forests, and refuges of Alaska, where grizzlies, caribou, Sitka black-tail deer, wolves, wolverines, moose, and Dall sheep ornament the valleys and mountains, and millions of birds cloud the skies. The BLM lands from eastern Oregon to southern New Mexico embrace a wealth of intermountain- and desert-grassland plant species. Whole populations of salmon species are disappearing from the river systems of the Pacific Northwest, but black-footed ferrets have been reintroduced to the Great Plains prairie, and "pothole" refuges have been created in North Dakota, where sandhill cranes gather to dance in the morning light.

Beyond question, the national lands are a great library of life, and we still have much to learn from them. The good news is that plenty of people are learning what the lands have to teach. At the private, non-profit Teton Science School in Moose, Wyoming, students ranging in age from ten to the golden years are introduced to ecological principles through field research in Grand Teton

RAYMOND GEHMAN

National Park and nearby national forests. Each year in California, as many as 5,000 students of the Yosemite Institute in Yosemite National Park use the park's resources to study everything from geological history to hydrological processes, while those at the Glacier Institute in Montana's Glacier National Park can attend field seminars on grizzly biology. In the East, children from Jersey City, New York, and Philadelphia can study the life and landscape in Delaware Water Gap National Recreation Area under the auspices of the Pocono Environmental Education Center. "They don't know anything about insect larvae, or salamanders, or tadpoles, or minnows," said one teacher at Delaware Water Gap of her students. "By the end of the course, they want to take them home. It turns what's on the pages into reality. These kids may stay inside the rest of their lives but they learn here that *their* environment depends in ways on *this* environment." For these students and many more like them, the national lands are a resource whose educational value is beyond measure.

In the same spirit, countless major research efforts are under way in national lands from the tundra of Cape Krusenstern National Monument in Alaska to the coral reefs of Virgin Islands National Park in the Caribbean. Many of these programs are sponsored by federal research and land-management agencies, some by major universities across the nation. However, most government scientists these days, whether they are National Park Service biologists trying to determine what is required for the "natural regulation" of animals in Yellowstone, or Marine Fisheries ichthyologists trying to keep fisheries from disappearing, find themselves working their way through a maze called "ecosystem management." In theory, ecosystem management calls for federal land managers to administer a piece of land so as to ensure its overall ecological health, with no single activity being allowed to damage the whole.

A noble intention, ecosystem management has evolved over the past 30 years or so and has proved difficult to implement. Nonetheless, it is now a required protocol among federal land managers. The discipline is being pursued with great vigor in the heart of Willamette National Forest in Oregon, one of those forests left fragmented by generations of intensive logging. To fly over much of this forest is to look down on one enormous clear-cut patch after another, a kind of arboreal mange that makes the heart sick. The sight raises the question of whether the remaining old-growth habitat in the Willamette and other Pacific Northwest forests can survive, even under a new presidentially-mandated plan to protect old growth.

Scientists at Andrews Experimental Forest in Willamette National Forest started to investigate this issue even before the controversy over the spotted owl made the old-growth forests of the Pacific Northwest a candidate for primetime TV back in the early 1990s. Beginning in 1970, with financing from a National Science Foundation grant and the participation of Oregon State University scientists, members of the H.J. Andrews Ecosystem Research Group began taking a close look at what made an old-growth forest tick. The researchers tested various logging techniques to determine the impact of timber-cutting on plant and animal life. They measured the diversity and range of animal species to determine the most healthy mix of tree species—age, size, spatial relationships—and dead and rotting logs that seemed necessary to preserve the biological mix of ecologically functional areas. Over time, the scientists have developed new approaches to managing forests and watersheds, built on the principles of ecosystem management.

THE JURY IS still out on the ultimate efficacy of this new approach. Even if ecosystem management develops into a well-defined and universally applied scientific method, many environmentalists doubt that it will be enough to reverse the tide of extinction and the dwindling of biodiversity. Indeed, some worry that even the current drift toward addressing ecological systems on a regionwide basis is not enough to halt gradual environmental degradation. Although mildly encouraged by the current debate, ecologist R. Edward Grumbine remains concerned. As he writes in *Ghost Bears: Exploring the Biodiversity Crisis*, "It is still too soon to tell what set of values ecosystem management will ultimately support. For, even though scientific ecosystem management may flourish in the coming years, biological diversity will not be sustained if new ways of managing nature do not also transform how we experience our place in nature, how we manage ourselves."

How we manage ourselves is indeed the longest of all the long-term environmental issues we must face as a nation. Through some measure of foresight and a lot of luck—and despite a plethora of mistakes—we are still shareholders in what remains an incomparable resource, the more than 630 million acres of national lands and the bounty of life they hold. These lands continue to be the very essence of our natural "capital," the ecological foundation on which human life and enterprise is built. But everywhere the lands are threatened by our careless enthusiasms, our seemingly unthinking devotion to consumption and uncontrolled growth, our everlasting need to measure our greatness as a people by what we can make the land do for us.

Owning these national lands is not enough. Managing them is not enough. Studying them is not enough. Perhaps even loving them is not enough. E. O. Wilson makes the case in *Biophilia* that "to explore and affiliate with life is a deep and complicated process in mental development. To an extent still undervalued in philosophy and religion, our existence depends on this propensity, our spirit is woven from it, hope rises on its currents." Honoring this connection to life—becoming truly deserving stewards of the gift of our national lands—may be our only hope of salvation as one more species in the great community.

FOLLOWING PAGES: *A mass of sun-hungry walrus bulls form a living carpet on an Alaskan beach in Togiak National Wildlife Refuge. In summer, the bulls gorge on mussels and clams to fatten up for their northward migration. Because low-flying airplanes can stampede the herds—injuring or killing some and causing the rest to waste needed energy— refuge staff have secured legal action, under the Marine Mammal Protection Act, against pilots who disturb the animals.*

JOEL SARTORE

TOWERING SNOWY HUMP *of Mount McKinley, 30 miles away, looms over Wonder Lake, where a silhouetted grizzly prowls the water's edge in Alaska's Denali National Park and Preserve. Sometimes*

MICHIO HOSHINO/MINDEN PICTURES

called the "Yellowstone of Alaska," Denali averages 340,000 visitors a year, yet it retains the wildness and connection to life that have inspired the establishment of our national lands system.

Author's Note

T. H. Watkins is the Wallace Stegner Distinguished Professor of Western American Studies at Montana State University in Bozeman, where he lives with his wife, Joan. A former senior editor of *American Heritage* magazine, he was editor of the Wilderness Society's *Wilderness* magazine for 16 years and is now a contributing editor to *Audubon*. In addition to his magazine work, he has also written numerous histories and environmental books, including *Righteous Pilgrim: The Life and Times of Harold L. Ickes, 1874–1952*, which won the *Los Angeles Times* Book Award for biography in 1991, and *Time's Island: The California Desert*.

Acknowledgments

The Book Division wishes to express its gratitude to the men and women of the U. S. Fish and Wildlife Service, the National Park Service, the Bureau of Land Management, and the Forest Service for their cooperation and assistance during the preparation of this book.

We also thank the many individuals, groups, and organizations mentioned or quoted in the text, as well as those cited here, for their help: Carolyn Alkire, Stephen Bailey, Bennett H. Beach, Sandy Berger, Bob Berrisford, David Blankinship, Ralph Bonde, Chris Brown, Ken Burton, Glenn Carowan, Timothy Cochrane, Christine Cowles, Dave Cowan, Cindy Daly, Michelle Dawson, Pam Druliner, Dabney Ford, Michael Francis, Daniel Gomez, John Greer, Scott Groene, Deb Guernsey, Bill Haglan, Jacquelyn Handly, John Hoogland, Dale Housley, Fran Hunt, Jeff Krauss, Denise Louie, Tim Manns, Cheryl Matthews, Fran Mauer, Kelly Mee, Jim Miller, Gary Muehlenhardt, John Myers, Linda Olson, Alan Polk, Norbert Riedy, Andy Ringgold, Lynn Rothgeb, Ellen Seeley, Beth Shimp, Steve Sorseth, Kathy Stark, Fred Swanson, Janet Tennyson, Laura Thompson-Olais, Tim Tibbitts, Paul Tritaik, Doug Vandegraft, Jim Waltman, Kathy Westlin, Charles T. Wilson, and Bill Wolverton; Defenders of Wildlife, the Greater Yellowstone Coalition, the Nature Conservancy, the Southern Utah Wilderness Alliance, the Wilderness Society, and the Yellowstone Wolf Project.

Additional Reading

The reader may wish to consult the *National Geographic Index* for related articles and books. The following titles may also be of interest:

Rocky Barker, *Saving All the Parts: Reconciling Economics and the Endangered Species Act;* Michael Cohen, *The History of the Sierra Club, 1892–1970;* Roger DiSilvestro, *The Endangered Kingdom: The Struggle to Save America's Wildlife;* Stephen Fox, *John Muir and His Legacy: The American Conservation Movement;* Frank Graham, *The Audubon Ark: A History of the National Audubon Society;* R. Edward Grumbine, *Ghost Bears: Exploring the Biodiversity Crisis;* Samuel P. Hayes, *Conservation and the Gospel of Efficiency;* Michael Hodgson, *America's Secret Recreation Areas: Your Recreation Guide to the Bureau of Land Management's Forgotten Wildlands of the West;* Hans Huth, *Nature and the American: Three Centuries of Changing Attitudes;* William MacLeish, *The Day Before America: Changing the Nature of a Continent;* Thomas McNamee, *The Return of the Wolf to Yellowstone;* Robert H. Mohlenbrock, *The Field Guide to U. S. National Forests;* Tim Palmer, *The Wild and Scenic Rivers of America;* Laura and William Riley, *Guide to the National Wildlife Refuges;* Jim Robbins, *Last Refuge: The Environmental Showdown in Yellowstone and the American West;* Roy Robbins, *Our Landed Heritage: The Public Domain, 1776–1970;* Alfred Runte, *National Parks: The American Experience;* Paul Schullery, *Searching for Yellowstone: Ecology and Wonder in the Last Wilderness;* Philip Shabecoff, *A Fierce Green Fire: The American Environmental Movement;* Wallace Stegner, *The American West as Living Space;* T. H. Watkins and Charles S. Watson, Jr., *The Lands No One Knows: America and the Public Domain;* Dyan Zaslowsky and T. H. Watkins, *These American Lands: Parks, Wilderness, and the Public Lands;* Charles I. Zinser, *Outdoor Recreation: United States National Parks, Forests, and Public Lands.*

INDEX

Boldface indicates illustrations.

Library of Congress CIP Data

Watkins, T. H. (Tom H.), 1936-
    Natural America / by T.H. Watkins.
        p.   cm.
    "Prepared by the Book Division,
    National Geographic Society."
    Includes index.
        ISBN 0-7922-7060-6 (reg.).—ISBN
    0-7922-7064-9 (dlx)
        1. Natural history—United States.
    2. Nature conservation—United States.
    I. National Geographic Society (U.S.).
    Book Division.   II. Title.
    QH104.W37 1998
    508.73—dc21   97-45239
                                              CIP

Composition for this book by the National Geographic Society Book Division with the assistance of the Typographic section of National Geographic Production Services, Pre-Press Division. Printed and bound by R. R. Donnelley & Sons, Willard, OH. Color separations by CMI Color Graphics, Inc., Huntingdon Valley, PA. Dust jacket printed by Miken Systems, Inc., Cheektowaga, NY.